BOOKS BY GEORGE D. PAINTER

ANDRÉ GIDE

ANDRÉ GIDE

A Critical Biography

GEORGE D. PAINTER

New York

ATHENEUM

To My Wife

FOREWORD

The original version of this book was written between 1948 and 1951, in the fervour and sense of revelation produced by a first and second reading of Gide's works. It was kindly received, soon went out of print, and is now revised and enlarged in the light of Gide's posthumous writings and other primary sources which have appeared since his death. There was much to correct, much to add; but the impressions under which it was written remain unaltered or constantly renewed today, sixteen years later. As Dr Germaine Brée has remarked in similar circumstances, 'my basic approach to Gide's work has not greatly changed. When I came back to his work I found that it was, rather, reaffirmed.' Gide is still the same, the more so now that 'eternity has changed him into himself'. The magnitude of his struggle and victory, the validity of his joy in youth and serenity in old age, are only corroborated by our increasing knowledge of the tensions that impelled him. As we climb the dark slope of the twentieth century this peak continues to rise behind us, in the sunlight, towards its true height.

It is true of every great writer, and particularly true of Gide, that his works are fashioned by the same inner conflicts that underlie his life. His books are complex living acts, his life becomes a work of art that includes his books. 'Each of his works is an action,' Gide wrote of Goethe, 'and conversely, his whole life seems a work of art, and one of the finest he created; I admire not only the flower, but the plant that bears it, and nourishes it, and from which we should not detach it.' He may have been thinking of himself as well as of Goethe, for Gide's is one of the great allegorical lives. Anti-mystic as he always believed himself to be, he underwent in youth the mystic experience of joy and liberation; and he devoted the rest of his long life to its preservation and purification, to its integration with the opposite principles of sacrifice and restraint, and to the search for a final harmony in which delight and abnegation, sense and spirit, demon and divinity, indulgence and sacrifice, would coexist and become one. His art is the means and end, the process, description and achievement of his quest.

A writer of genius offers us primarily not a doctrine (for to any doctrine a hostile answer is always available), nor even a harmonious spectacle, but a significant experience, his own. To understand him it is necessary to undergo that experience, and to criticize him it is necessary to remain at least half-immersed in it at the time of writing. No critic will ever succeed in getting the best of Gide, who has not first renounced all desire to get the better of him.

I have tried to approach Gide's works through the living mind that created them, to describe not only their actual nature and content, but their organic growth from the history of that mind and heart. He was, I think, the last great writer of our age, and also the most salutary. He has no equal in this century as a giver of sheer pleasure, aesthetic, intellectual and sensory; but he is even more important as a source of spiritual joy, as a heroic guide in the acquisition of personal happiness, virtue, and liberty.

CONTENTS

ILLUSTRATIONS

The author and publishers are grateful to the owners for permission to reproduce
the photographs.

Photographic research: Françoise Foliot, Paris.

ANDRÉ GIDE

INFANCY
AND SCHOOLDAYS

The Notebooks of André Walter

'I am a little boy at play, combined with a Protestant clergyman who bores him.' – *Journal*, 22 June 1907.

André Gide was born in Paris on 22 November 1869, to Paul Gide, Professor in the Faculty of Law at the Sorbonne, and his wife Juliette. They lived in a top-floor flat in the Rue de Médicis, from whose balcony the boy André would launch paper darts, and watch them sailing over the square and the fountain, till caught in the tall chestnut-trees of the Luxembourg Gardens. Two other memories, both unseemly, belong to the Rue de Médicis: André played dubious games under the dining-room table with the caretaker's son, and in the Gardens he trod on the sand pies of the other children, because they refused to play with him. A photograph of this period shows him 'wearing an absurd check frock, and cowering in my mother's skirts, with a sickly, hostile air and shifty gaze.'

Gide's father came of a Protestant family in Uzès, a small town in the south of France, near Nîmes, and a nest of Huguenots since the Reformation. Grandfather Tancrède, after retiring from chairmanship of the local bench, devoted himself entirely to good works, including moral and religious instruction at the Uzès Sunday-school. He had died before the birth of André, refusing to commit the impiety of sending for a doctor. He was an austere, inflexible old bigot, whose angular disposition extended to other members of the family, but missed Gide's father. Yet to his superiors he had seemed unsuitable for his post, owing to his excessive kindliness and his scrupulous adhesion to the command: 'Judge not, that ye be not judged'; and these were qualities later shared by his grandson both as writer and as juryman.

In 1863 Paul Gide had married Juliette Rondeaux, a rich heiress of Rouen. Her father, Édouard Rondeaux, a Freemason's son and a Voltairean rationalist though a Catholic born, had taken a Protestant wife, and allowed his children to be brought up in the religion of their mother. In this union of north and south, of the wine and almond-trees and scorched heaths of the Midi with the cider and apple-trees and sunless woods of Normandy, Gide always saw the source or symbol of the twin polarities of his nature, and of his need to reconcile them through the work of art. He was to begin a review of Barrès's regionalist novel, *Les Déracinés* (*The Uprooted*), with a famous sentence: 'Born in Paris, of a father from Uzès and a mother from Normandy, where, M. Barrès, would you have me take root?' And yet the similarity of the two strains in his blood is more striking than their differences. From both families came the same Protestant heritage of self-sacrifice and moral fervour, harsher perhaps on his father's side, more patient and cultured, but no less domineering, on his mother's. But there is no need to imagine some unknown rebellious ancestor to account for Gide. Impulses of joy and liberty, accumulated and pressed down by other generations, exploded in him to consciousness and freedom.

In 1875 the family moved to the Rue de Tournon, which runs into the Rue de Vaugirard opposite the Luxembourg Palace. In the new apartment his father had a huge gloomy study, into which he would invite André and with him trace the wormholes from page to page of some legal folio. He took the child for walks in the streets of Paris: 'Will my little friend come for a stroll with me?' he would say. And he read to him, instead of the inept children's books of the period, from the *Arabian Nights*, the *Odyssey*, Molière, or the farce of Pathelin. At this time André preferred his father to his mother. She exacted instant obedience – 'The Hebrews had to live under the law before they found grace,' she said – and André was insubordinate. But his father, blessed with a sweetness of disposition unique on his side of the family, could obtain anything he wished from him with a word.

At the age of five André attended a private school for infant boys and big girls. While he struggled over his alphabet, he enviously watched the girls wearing false beards, as they rehearsed for a performance of Racine's *Les Plaideurs*. At seven he began piano lessons with Mlle de Goecklin, who was too poor to eat, but owned a cage of tropical birds and a piano that was never in tune. 'We shall have to send for the tuner,' she would say; but the tuner never came. And at eight years old he went to the partly Protestant École Alsacienne in the Rue d'Assas, at the other side of the Luxembourg. 'I was still asleep, like a creature unborn,' he confesses. 'Hazel and nut-tree are synonyms,' the master told the class. 'Now, Gide, of what is hazel a synonym?' – and Gide could not answer. However, it was not for this crime (which only earned him 'nought for conduct') that his parents were asked to withdraw him for a term, but for 'bad habits,' which he took no trouble to conceal, having no idea as yet that they were reprehensible. Measles lost him another term. Next year, being obliged to begin again in the same form, he found lessons easy, and acquired a taste for work.

His mother, in order that no one, particularly André himself, should be painfully aware of their difference in fortune, made him dress in the same style as his poorer friends. Unfortunately his friends' mothers cared neither for beauty nor comfort in dress. He would have liked a sailor suit with a beret: he was forced to wear knee-breeches, striped stockings, and a ridiculous miniature bowler hat. 'And I had to wait till I was almost a grown man,' he laments, 'before I was allowed to wear a soft shirt.' Carnival-time approached, and the mothers consulted a list of fancy-dresses for hire, ranging in diminuendo from little lord, through punchinello and bandit, to pastry-cook. Nothing was cheaper than this last, which consisted of a white calico suit with apron – decidedly André and his friend Julien must go to the ball as pastry-cooks. They looked like a pair of pocket-handkerchiefs. André fell in love with a little boy dressed as an imp in black tights and spangles; but, alas, there was nothing that could distinguish him to this marvel from the host of other little boys whose mothers had dressed them as pastry-cooks. Such was André's despair that his mother promised he should go next year as a bandit: so he did, but the imp in spangles was not there.

Easter holidays were spent at Uzès with Grandmother Gide, who knitted endless pairs of socks and left them unfinished about the house. Her daughter-in-law Anna, wife of André's Uncle Charles Gide, the economist, once asked her brutally: 'Why do you never finish any, Grandmother?' And the old lady answered, much hurt, 'Finish them, finish them – really, Anna – that takes time.' In the larder door André found a knot-hole, in which he felt, with his finger, something round and hard. It was a marble which his father had put there when a child, the servant told him, and no one had ever been able to get it out. Next summer André let his finger-nail grow, and immediately on arrival at Uzès, ran to the larder, and extracted the hidden treasure. It was only an ordinary marble: disappointed, he slid it back again, told no one, and trimmed his finger-nail.

For the summer holidays they went to La Roque, a property in Normandy bought by Gide's maternal grandfather, and inherited by his mother. The house was surrounded by a moat – what a joy to live on an island! – where André fished for trout, and watched the swallows that glided twittering round the house, cutting the blue of the sky in fine weather, skimming the water in time of coming rain. Round about grew pathless woods – André postponed as long as possible the day when he first discovered they were not endless, that ordinary fields lay on the other side.

The New Year holiday was spent in Rouen, where André stayed with Catholic Uncle Henri Rondeaux, and played with his cousins Jeanne, Valentine, and Madeleine, daughters of his Uncle Émile, the Protestant. Uncle Émile lived in the Rue de Lecat, as had the parents of Flaubert before him, and owned a country house at Cuverville, in whose garden was a huge cedar-tree. When André climbed with Jeanne to its topmost branches the two children could see, on clear days, ten miles away, the silver line of the sea. André preferred Jeanne to Madeleine: Jeanne was resolute and bold: she could climb trees, and, without sharing his passion for entomology, was willing to join him in turning over cow-dung and carrion in search of beetles for his collecting-bottle. Madeleine was two years older than André; she was a quiet, timid girl, and would hide herself away with a book when the games of the others became too noisy. Also with them at Rouen was Miss Anna Shackleton, orphan daughter of a Scottish iron-founder who had helped in building the railway from Paris to Le Havre. She had been the governess of André's mother, and remained her friend. She loved German literature, and would read to André from her own translations of Goethe; but her favourite study was botany. She took André with her on Sunday excursions in the country near Paris, organized by the Natural History Museum of the Jardin des Plantes. With this band of (as Gide calls them) old maids and amiable lunatics, she collected plants for her herbal; but André specialized in beetles. His passion for natural history began early. In a letter to his father, when the child was four years old, his mother wrote: 'André would be very nice, if he didn't have a mania for standing absolutely still at the foot of a tree watching snails.'

In 1880 André's father died of intestinal tuberculosis. For a long time the boy imagined that his father was dead only in the day-time: that at night, somehow, he returned, and stayed till morning in his mother's bedroom. Now only André was left for his mother to love; and her love closed round him with a domination and apprehension she had neither needed nor dared to show towards her husband. André's school-life was again interrupted. The time of mourning was spent at Rouen and La Roque, where he shared his cousins' tutor. For New Year's gift he was given a hectograph, and started a family magazine. Ought we to find here the begin-nings of his vocation as a writer? No – his cousins contributed original verse and prose, but André made extracts from Buffon and Boileau, thinking these would give his elders more pleasure than anything he could compose himself.

Next year, concern for André's health, or perhaps the lonely unsettledness of widowhood, brought Mme Gide to Montpellier, where his father's brother Charles was Professor in the Faculty of Law at the University. His new school-fellows persecuted him for his Protestant heresy. His parents had kept him unaware of the existence of two faiths in France, and the revelation had first come at his first playtime at the École Alsacienne, where a group had surrounded him and elegantly demanded, 'Are you Catholic or Protestarse (*Protescul*)?' But at Montpellier his minority status became more serious. Every day he was chased home by a howling mob, and reached his horrified mother covered with mud and bleeding at the nose. In his dreams he saw his chief tormentor, the appalling Gomez, and smelled the dead cat this monster had rubbed in his face. An attack of chicken-pox mercifully released him; and when it was time for him to return to school, he invented a fainting-fit, and then a whole repertoire of hysterical seizures. These fits began as play-acting and became real. Though he exaggerated them, he grew unable to prevent them entirely, and they relaxed, as nothing else would, the tension of his nerves, the terror and misery of the realization he had announced, a year or two before, in a storm of weeping, to his mother: 'I am not like other people; I am not like other people!' Often, in later years, he regretted the time when a few kicks and spasms would have brought relief! Three doctors were called into consultation, and pronounced his complaint authentic. But his Uncle Charles remained unimpressed. One day André awaited his approach, supine on the floor under a table. His uncle, buried in a newspaper, was about to pass without noticing: André stirred and groaned. 'What on earth are you doing there?' his uncle inquired. 'I am in pain!' But his uncle, unmoved, resumed his reading and returned to his library. André was much annoyed, not realizing as yet that his uncle always refused to take seriously the illnesses of other people.

The summer and autumn were spent in taking carbonic acid baths at Lamalou, a nearby spa. In the winter André returned to Paris and the École Alsacienne. After a fortnight of boredom, hysteria was replaced by another malady more serviceable at school. He was afflicted with headaches, mental fatigue, and insomnia, which an idiotic doctor treated with bromide and chloral. At night a tumbler of chloral stood at the twelve-year-old boy's bedside; at meals he drank a syrup of orange juice and potassium bromide. It tasted so delicious, that it was a wonder he ever succeeded in breaking the habit. This regime brought André to the verge of imbecility. The headaches lasted until his twentieth year, and returned in 1916, when he was no longer given to feigning illness: perhaps, he decided, they had not been so artificial as he believed.

The New Year was spent as usual at Rouen with his cousins. Madeleine had grown, matured beyond her years by a hidden grief, and the discovery of her secret was the chief event of André's early years, a revelation which altered the whole course of his life. He returned one evening from visiting Uncle Émile's family, and finding his mother not yet home, decided to go back and take his cousins by surprise. No one was about. He stole upstairs to Madeleine's room, and found her kneeling at her bedside, in tears. 'I felt that all my life and all my love would be needed to cure the enormous, intolerable sorrow which dwelt in her. I had discovered the mystic orientation of my life.' Madeleine's burden was indeed heavy for a girl so young and pure: she must bear the knowledge of her mother's infidelity, a secret which all Rouen knew and laughed about, and only her father and sisters had not yet discovered. Soon after, her mother fled with her lover, whom she married after her divorce; and Madeleine, all her life, felt a horror of fleshly love.

On their return to Paris Mme Gide moved to a larger apartment at 4 Rue de Commailles. It had a carriage entrance, for 'It is not a matter of convenience, but of decency,' Aunt Claire Démarest said, 'You owe it to yourself and your son.' The next few years passed with a succession of seedy tutors and burlesque piano-teachers. In 1883 Mme Gide took André to piano recitals by Rubinstein and concerts by the Pasdeloup Orchestra, in 1884 to the theatre, and in 1885, when he was sixteen, at the instigation of Cousin Albert Démarest, he was at last given the freedom of his dead father's library. The image of his cousin Madeleine followed him everywhere in his reading. Opposite every passage which seemed to deserve their joint admiration, astonishment, or love, he wrote her initials in the margin; and he had begun a regular correspondence with her. Their discovery of Homer and Æschylus, in the severe and magnificent translation of Leconte de Lisle, coincided with his reading of the Bible in preparation for his first communion. Yet there seemed no conflict between the sacred writings of Greeks and Hebrews: the beauty he sought in either was the same. He was disappointed to find no response to his ardour in the worthy but boring Protestant minister whose preparation course he followed for two years. He craved for admission to the divine mysteries, and Pastor Couve showed him only the voyages of St Paul. But he read the New Testament everywhere, even at morning break at school, ignoring the mockery of his comrades. The ceremony of first communion, so official and formal, gave him nothing new; but in the Gospels he saw the explanation and authorization of his love for Madeleine. He drew up and kept a time-table for his studies. He rose at dawn, took a cold bath, slept on boards, and awoke at dead of night to kneel and pray; and in these exercises he saw an act not of mortification, but of joy. But perhaps, he realized later, his love for his cousin, like his love for God, depended on the absence of the Beloved. Perhaps, he said, during these ardent renunciations of the flesh, he might have heard – if only he had listened – the Devil rubbing his hands and sniggering in the corner!

In October 1887 he returned at last to the École Alsacienne. During the past eighteen months he had studied under three excellent teachers. Under Marc de la Nux, a pupil of Liszt, he was fast becoming a virtuoso at the piano. At the boarding-school of the Protestant Jacob Keller, and in the summers at La Roque under the tutorship of Pastor Élie Allégret, he had made up the five years lost in truancy since his father's death. At the École Alsacienne, rather to his horror, he soon took the place of the brilliant Pierre Louÿs[1] in the weekly French composition. When the master first announced to the stupefied class, 'First, Gide. Second, Louÿs, Gide felt that any hope of winning Pierre's friendship was lost. Louÿs had turned pale, and was sharpening a pencil with an air of unconcern. But soon afterwards he found Gide reading Heine's *Book of Songs* in the original German. 'Why, do you like poetry?' he exclaimed, with unflattering surprise: and with the discovery of this common interest the two became inseparable

[1] At this time he was still Pierre Louis, and had not yet invented the symbolist spelling of his pen-name, Louÿs.

companions. Gide introduced Louÿs to his mother, who found him 'very well brought up, quite a distinguished boy.' They exchanged poems during Sunday walks in the Bois de Meudon, and Gide apologized for the deficiencies of his own verses by explaining that his whole heart was devoted to a future prose work, *Les Cahiers d'André Walter* (*The Notebooks of André Walter*). And he confessed his love for his cousin, of which *André Walter* was to be a declaration so noble and moving that, surely, it would win her heart, and the consent of their relatives to their marriage.

The teaching at the École Alsacienne was supposed to be inadequate for the final year of philosophy. Louÿs moved to the Lycée Janson-de-Sailly and Gide to the Lycée Henri IV. He remained only for a term, and then persuaded his mother that he could do still better by private reading. He found time to join Louÿs and Marcel Drouin in launching a school magazine, *Potache-Revue*, to which he contributed 'some rain-coloured stanzas' under the *Arabian Nights* pseudonym of Zan-bal-dar. In July 1889 he sat for his baccalaureate and was ploughed; in October he tried again and scraped through. As a reward he was allowed to take a walking-tour in Brittany, but not alone: his mother went on ahead, and their route was planned so that every few days he should join her. He shared the inn at Pouldu with a party of noisy artists. Their canvases, stacked against the wall of the dining-room, seemed childish daubs, yet with a strange life and joy in their colouring. He looked in the visitors' book for the names of these amusing eccentrics; all were unknown; one was named Paul Gauguin.

In February 1890 Pierre Louÿs wrote to a friend that Gide was about to begin his great work, 'though his family thinks he is studying for his licentiate in philosophy. Of all our friends he has the most future. I wish I might one day have the prose style he has now.' Next month Gide retired to Pierrefonds, a village complete with castle and lake on the southern edge of the Forest of Compiègne, to write *André Walter*. It was too near Paris. After two days Pierre Louÿs descended upon him, full of advice as irritating as his banter. Gide fled to Switzerland and settled at Menthon on the Lake of Annecy. In this solitude he was able to maintain 'the state of lyrical fervour without which I thought it unseemly to write.'

By the end of summer he was back in Paris, reading the completed *André Walter* to his cousin Albert Démarest, who persuaded him to delete two-thirds of the quotations from the Bible: 'how many there were, you may judge from the number that remain.'

André Walter[1] is a devout young Protestant of nineteen, in love with his orphan cousin and adoptive sister Emmanuèle.[2] His dying mother has persuaded herself that her son's love is fraternal only, and, to save them both from an unhappy marriage, makes him promise to renounce his cousin. She then betroths Emmanuèle to another, and the three young people kneel and pray at her bedside.[3] Six months later Emmanuèle marries, and André Walter begins to write. First comes the 'White Notebook', colour of renunciation and chastity. He retraces the growth of his love for his cousin, how they visited the poor together and prayed side by side over a dead child, how they rode back from Le Havre on the outside seat of the family carriage, reciting verses and falling asleep hand in hand. By the menhirs on the sea-cliff they watched the lighthouses beginning one by one to flash. He read aloud to her, sometimes alone with her in the linen-room, while she folded the linen, sometimes in the lamplight of the family circle – but even then, as he read from Hoffmann or Turgenev, his voice 'had inflexions for her alone.' Or they would read Homer, Heine, Spinoza, Dante, together, sitting at the table with the book between them. And once (Gide recalls here that day of dedication in Madeleine's room at the Rue Lecat) he finds her in her room, in tears. Spring passes as he writes, bringing new desires, which he successfully resists; by summer his renunciation is complete. 'Since I must lose her, may I regain Thee, my God, and Thy blessing that I have followed the strait path.' But as he commences his novel

---

[1] The source of the name is significant. Mme Henriette André-Walther, 1807–1886, was a prominent Protestant and evangelical worker, whose biography by her son had been published in 1889.

[2] Gide continued to use this emblematic pseudonym for his cousin and wife Madeleine in his autobiography and *Journal*. In a few copies of the first edition of *André Walter*, it is said, the heroine's name was given as Madeleine.

[3] It was not long since Gide and his cousin had in fact watched together over a parent's deathbed – that of her father, Gide's uncle Émile Rondeaux, who died in March 1890.

'*Allain*,' news comes of the death of Emmanuèle. His sacrifice has been in vain.

He begins the 'Black Notebook', colour of mourning and despair. Emmanuèle returns to him in dreams that border on hallucination. '*Allain*' is to be the story of an inner conflict between the Angel and the Beast, the soul and the body, which will end in the hero's insanity. 'It is a race between us which shall go mad first, Allain or myself,' Walter writes wildly: Allain wins the race, but his creator and double is not far behind. André Walter falls ill of brain fever, that legendary disease of the late nineteenth century, which was thought a natural consequence of mental stress and disappointed love. 'I must say it was very kind,' he writes in his last journal entry, not long before his death: 'Emmanuèle watched all night at my bedside, and gave me drinks when I was thirsty. At first I did not recognize her – how odd, I had thought she was dead! We laughed over it together when I told her.' Snow is falling outside – or does he imagine this too? The whiteness of charity and sacrifice has brought him to the whiteness of death, the cold of outer space. 'How white the snow is ... how pure.'

André Walter was to Gide what '*Allain*' was to André Walter: a book into which he put his whole world of spirit and flesh, all his youth of religion, books, and love. He saw it not as the first step in a literary career, but as an end in itself, beyond which lay perhaps the madness and death that had overtaken his hero. But his novel also served a much more practical purpose. It was a declaration of love to his cousin, an appeal to their shared experience of literature and piety, and a warning of the possible consequences of denying a union that, in the spirit, seemed already an accomplished fact. And it was an act of rebellion and revenge against his mother, an attempt to escape, through the mental hygiene of a work of art, from her destructive domination. True, Walter obeys his mother, but her coercion costs the deaths of his cousin and himself, and is immediately punished by her own. How different, five years later, was real life to be! For Mme Gide was to die, leaving Gide in possession both of his most lawless desires and of his cousin. But for the time being *André Walter* failed to produce the desired effect upon Madeleine Rondeaux. She refrained from telling him her opinion of his book, but she refused the proposal of marriage which accompanied it, and ceased to answer his letters.

Consciously wounded by this rejection, though perhaps also unconsciously relieved, Gide travelled in the next five years a path which led away from his cousin. Her refusal had freed him from her restraint, and he set out to explore the other side of his nature. In his life and writings he advanced towards liberation through the senses, and the gradual discovery, first painful, then joyful, of his own homosexuality. But he was also impelled by the almost incompatible wishes to punish his cousin through hostile irony and the spectacle of his disarray, and to regain her love by demonstrating the greatness of her loss in withholding it. It is not surprising that Madeleine Rondeaux disapproved even more strongly of his next works, in which all these themes are visible, than of *André Walter*. In the summer of 1892 their meetings and letters were to begin again, too late for their salvation in this world. 'I repeat the prayer I used to say for you when I was a little girl,' she wrote to him then, '"Give me faith, O God, increase André's faith, and teach him to be gentle and humble of heart" – and I used to add: "Grant that we may love each other always." But I have ceased to make this last request.' Of *The Poems of André Walter* she remarked: 'Very boring and very bad. I assure you that you did not take long to descend from the pedestal – oh, a very small pedestal – on which the *Notebooks* and the *Narcissus* had perched you.'

In his preface to the new edition of 1930 Gide became his first book's severest critic. 'Nothing pains me more, on re-reading my *André Walter*, than the complaisance towards myself that makes every phrase so insipid. Often what I took for the sincerest expression of myself was only the outcome of my puritan education, which, by teaching me to fight against my secret longings, satisfied in me a taste for spiritual combat and specious austerity. I consider André Walter a very bad example,' he concludes, 'and his notebooks give rather poor advice.' Naturally, for André Walter is a young man who goes mad through renunciation, and Gide was to learn that renunciation and enjoyment are equally necessary, equally healthy and natural. Walter's bad example lies in his inability to practise both, just as Gide's Immoralist was to go mad, or as good as mad, for the opposite fault, for enjoying without renunciation.

To think too highly of *André Walter* would be to throw the rest of Gide's writings out of proportion. It is a remarkable work for a young man of twenty, but it is a work of precocity, not of genius. Paragraph by paragraph, lyrically and philosophically, it may be pleasurably meditated over: as a whole, it is nearly unreadable. No one could predict from it that Gide would ever know how to tell a story, or to achieve beauty of form. The structure of *The Notebooks* is not so much complex as chaotic. André Walter moves without signposts between past and present: his extracts from a former journal[1] make a diary within a diary, '*Allain*' is a novel within a novel; and the result is a bewildering farrago. 'Take care of your form,' Pierre Louÿs had urged; 'without it your ideas will be understood only by your contemporaries – it is by form that a book lives.' And he advised, equally in vain, that Walter should be objectified, 'shown in broad daylight', made 'a type, but a living one.' But Gide wished to remove any element of contingency by making his characters, scenes, and events as general as possible. 'No external sign of the inner drama must appear, no facts, no images, except perhaps symbolic ones.' The sterility of this principle in *André Walter* revealed to him the truth of the paradox, that a work of art is universal in direct proportion to its particularity.

[1] These are the only surviving relics of the journal Gide began in 1887 and later destroyed. His published *Journals* begin in 1889.

2

THE SYMBOLIST
HOTHOUSE

*The Treatise of the Narcissus, The Voyage of Urien,
The Attempt at Love, Marshlands*

'The garden of symbolism opens at our feet, with its flowers
and scents. There is no way out.' – *Valéry to Gide*, March 1891.

Gide and Louÿs had made a compact that each should contribute
a page to the other's first book. 'I felt he was as incapable of writing a page of my prose as I of writing one of his sonnets,' said
Gide; and in the end Louÿs wrote only an ironically respectful
preface to *André Walter*, lamenting the early death of his promising
young friend. To continue the fiction *André Walter* appeared, in
January 1891, anonymously, in a de luxe edition of two hundred
copies, and in a cheap edition[1] intended to meet an imaginary
popular demand. So few were buyers of the latter, and so numerous the misprints, that Gide at last called at the binders with a
cab, and carried off the remainder of the edition to be pulped; he
accepted with melancholy pleasure the amount of its value as
wastepaper.

But Louÿs insisted on introducing his friend's book in more
ways than one. Louÿs was by now an intimate at Mallarmé's
Tuesdays and Heredia's Saturdays, where he introduced Gide to
the giants and dwarfs of symbolism and parnassianism. He in-
structed Gide in the principles of what he called *auto-lançage*, or
self-publicity: 'never ask for anything; make everyone think you

[1] On the wrapper is a vignette of a winged mermaid, with the inscription *Non
hic piscis omnibus* – 'This isn't everybody's fish!'

need the help of no one', and so on. Under his guidance Gide, with growing nausea, hawked his book from genius to genius. What a revenge was preparing under his mask of deferential gratitude! The end came when, having run out of celebrities, he began the round of the nonentities. 'What, visit Vanot?' cried Henri de Régnier, 'Why, he'll boast about it for the rest of his life.' And Gide made and kept a vow to 'withdraw himself from success'.

Meanwhile compliments flowed in from all the great writers of the age: for a friend's friend they could hardly do less. Mallarmé, Huysmans, Maeterlinck, Barrès, Bourget, Marcel Schwob, wrote letters of unanimous praise. 'At moments *André Walter* is eternal, like *The Imitation of Christ*,' said Maeterlinck. 'I wish we could salute a new prince of literature *every* January,' said Barrès. Régnier, Maurras, Gourmont wrote articles comparing *André Walter* to *Werther, Dominique*, and Sainte-Beuve's *Volupté*. Redonnel sounded a discordant note: 'I am told Barrès has fallen for it; I am hardly surprised.' Gourmont made a remarkably shrewd prophecy: 'One day this author will recognize the impotence of pure thought on the march of things, the scorn it inspires in the heap of corpuscles called society; and he will awaken armed with irony.'

Gide had recently made, again through Louÿs, a friendship of more lasting importance than these temporary handshakes. At the celebration in June 1890 of the sexcentenary of the University of Montpellier, Louÿs had met a young poet of that town, Paul Valéry,[1] an enthusiast for Poe and Mallarmé. In December Gide, recommended by Louÿs, himself visited Valéry, a visit followed by an ardent correspondence and Gide's temporary immersion in Mallarmé and the symbolists. 'When I met you,' he wrote to Valéry (26th January 1891), 'I was an impassioned critic of "your school" – now all their theories seem a direct apologia of my book – so now it is Mallarmé for poetry, Maeterlinck for the drama, and Me for the novel.' More amazing still, not content with finding himself, unawares, a symbolist novelist, Gide became a

[1] Louÿs' brother Georges wrote to him: 'I hope you will not de-Gide yourself,' and Louÿs replied: 'When I Valéryse I do not de-Gide, on the contrary!'

symbolist poet. In a little over a week he produced the twenty delicious but ironical lyrics of *Les Poésies d'André Walter*, in which Walter ('these poems are too good for him,' said Gide later) recalls the summers spent with Emmanuèle before his mother died. His next work also was inspired by emulation with Valéry. They had walked together in the public gardens of Montpellier by the cenotaph, inscribed *Placandis Narcissæ manibus* (For the peace of Narcissa's soul), of the daughter of the English poet Young (he who wrote *Night Thoughts*). Narcissa's shade called up Narcissus. Valéry produced his miraculous alexandrines, *Narcisse parle*; Gide the prose *Le Traité du Narcisse (Treatise of the Narcissus)*, dedicated to Valéry.[1]

André Walter's posthumous poems and the *Treatise* were the only children of Gide's symbolist honeymoon. Narcissus in search of a mirror, not so much for his face as for his soul, leans over the river of time, as it hurries from the future, past the present where Narcissus gazes, downstream to the past. It flows from and to the Earthly Paradise, timeless home of the ideal[2], where Adam, sexless and bored, plucked a branch from the tree Ygdrasil and was expelled, to know the imperfection of love and the search for lost truth. And Narcissus, attempting in vain to embrace his own image in the water, decides that a symbol can never be possessed: it must be contemplated only. This eminently symbolist solution did not content Gide for long. The symbolists were only too successful in conveying that all things are symbols—but of what, they could not or would not discover. The real obscurity of Mallarmé lies not in the density of his thought, but in its lack of an object – his poems tend not to be about anything. His weaving of the images that veil truth cost him the forward energy that would have enabled him to break through. Valéry, in his greatest poems, *La Jeune Parque* and *Le Cimetière marin*, was to transcend symbolism

---

[1] By a curious coincidence Gide had already thought of the title in the previous May, before he had even heard of Valéry, and Valéry had already written in September an early version of his poem in sonnet form.

[2] An idea in which Gide not only borrows from Plato but also approaches, for a never-repeated instant, the Time Regained of Proust. Gide and Proust were both in search of the same, the eternal truth; but Gide went forward, Proust backward, to seize it.

Gide, aged 3, with his mother, 1872 (*Collection Mme Catherine Lambert Gide*)

Gide, aged 6, in 1875 (*Collection Mme Catherine Lambert Gide*)

Gide's father, Paul Gide (*Collection Mme Catherine Lambert Gide*)

Gide's mother, Juliette Gide (*Collection Mme Catherine Lambert Gide*)

Gide and classmates at École Alsa
cienne, 1877 (*Collection Mme Catherine
Lambert Gide*)

Gide in 1891 (*Bibliothèque Jacques
Doucet*)

by his conviction that the truth, whatever it may be, is not only intellectual and artistic, but moral, and a moral effort is needed to attain it. And so it was with Gide. He entered the 'symbolist hothouse' in search of release from the moral tension of *André Walter*, and found only a lull. The air which the others were content to breathe all their lives, suffocated him. People who live in a glass house . . . he emerged, and bombarded it from outside, aided, once more, by a timely new acquaintance.

Oscar Wilde was now enjoying the splendid maturity that came between his spring of self-sought ridicule and his winter of self-sought ruin. No longer Bunthorne, not yet Melmoth, he was, in his own phrase, the King of Life. In November 1891 he descended on Paris. Gide heard of him at Mallarmé's and procured an invitation to dine with him. Wilde, brilliant but guarded, was taking stock. After dinner he said to Gide: 'You hear with your eyes – that is why I am going to tell you this story.' And he told the parable of the River that loved Narcissus[1] because it could see in his eyes the reflection of its waters. 'I do not like your lips,' he told Gide, 'they are quite straight, like the lips of one who has never told a lie.' Beginning immediately after Wilde's visit, signs of a coming moral thaw appear in Gide's journal. At first he struggles against the new influence; then, gradually, he is converted. 'Wilde, I think, has done me nothing but harm. I have unlearned how to think. My emotions are more diverse, but I can no longer set them in order.' 'I am harried by this dilemma: how to be both moral and sincere.' 'Happiness is a duty.' 'O God, grant that my prison of morality may burst open, that I may live fully, and without fear, without believing that I am going to sin.' But he is still unaware of his physical destiny.[2] 'At twenty-three I am completely virgin, and depraved thereby.' 'It would be a joy to feel oneself robust and *normal*. I live in hope.'

Gide's second novel, *Le Voyage d'Urien*, was not published until August 1893. But its final chapter appeared separately in December

[1] Either this is a remarkable coincidence, or he had read Gide's *Treatise of the Narcissus*, and was doubly relating his parable to his listener.

[2] 'At no time during our intimacy [before 1895] did he [Wilde] give me the slightest ground for suspicion' – or so Gide affirms.

1892 under the title 'A Journey to Spitzbergen', and Gide hastened
to present it to Mallarmé. The master accepted it with a frown, but
at their next meeting he greeted Gide with an exquisite smile. 'You
gave me such a fright,' he said, 'I was afraid you had really been
there.' Mallarmé's apprehension was in fact needless, for Urien's
voyage on the good ship *Orion* is as imaginary as are his nineteen
companions with the euphonious names.[1] Its fabulous landscapes
are those of Rimbaud's '*Bateau Ivre*' and of Jules Verne's *Twenty
Thousand Leagues Under the Sea*; its cities of mirage come from
Salammbo, its horrors from Poe; and, like Poe's *Arthur Gordon
Pym*, *The Voyage of Urien* is a journey to a miraculous Pole. Part
One, 'A Voyage on the Pathetic Ocean', brings a series of temptations, increasingly overt, to heterosexual pleasure. In the palace of
the vampire queen Haïatalnefus, eight 'false knights' succumb,
only to be destroyed, with their female accomplices, by a ghastly
plague. The twelve apostles of purity ('feeling very vividly what
we wished not to be, we began to understand what in fact we
were') survive for a well-deserved sojourn in the Sargasso of
ennui, where the *Orion* shrinks into a small felucca.[2] They ascend
a melancholy river in the weed, on whose banks smoke-coloured
herons fish for mudworms. And there waiting for them, having
come by the land route; wearing a pea-green gown, with a tartan
shawl and a cherry-red sunshade; eating an endive salad and reading *Prolegomena to Any Future Metaphysic*, is Urien's 'dear Ellis'.
'The meeting was rather joyless, and owing to the different routes
we had followed, we found nothing to say; for we had acquired
the habit of talking only about things which we both knew.'
Ellis persists in her habit of reading, and still worse, she infects the
others. One morning Urien finds his comrades sitting on the bank
reading moral pamphlets distributed by Ellis. 'Don't you realize,
wretched Ellis,' he cries, 'that books are temptations? And we set

[1] Alain, Paride, Nathanael, Mélian, Tradelineau, Agloval, Angaire, Cabilor,
Morgain, Odinel, Lambègue, Alfasar, Hector, Ydier, Axel, Clarion, Aguisel,
Eric, Hélain. Angaire is Valéry, Cabilor is Pierre Louÿs, Ydier is Drouin, Tradelineau is Maurice Quillot, Alain is André Walter, and no doubt, did we but know,
others of these names conceal other heroes of symbolism and Parnassus.

[2] Cf. the phantom ship in Poe's *MS. Found in a Bottle*, which, on the contrary,
grows.

out for glorious deeds!' And he hurls her bag, which still contains a *Life of Franklin*, a concise flora of the temperate zone and Paul Desjardins's *Le Devoir présent* into the water.[1] 'Ellis had understood nothing; I recognized this from the irritation I suddenly felt against her.' They redescend the mysterious river. Urien examines his face reflected in the black water, and reads 'in the curve of my lips[2] the bitterness of the regret that curves them. Ellis! do not read this, these lines are not written for you! You could never understand the despair of my soul.' Ellis takes fever and becomes 'vaguely delirious'; and a terrible doubt seizes Urien. The Ellis he knew was a brunette – and this is a blonde! 'Ellis,' Urien tells her, 'you have become an obstacle to my fusion with God, and I shall only be able to love you if you too become merged in Him.' And when they maroon poor Ellis on the shore, and set out over the icy sea to the Pole, she has 'almost lost all reality.' 'I do not care for sentimental melancholies,' Urien remarks.

The travellers develop scurvy and are cured by the Eskimos. The Polar night descends and the sea freezes. They make a sledge from the wood of their ship, burn the rest, and march on.[3] While his comrades sleep, the real Ellis, the brunette, appears to Urien. 'I thought one day I had found you on the river bank,' he tells her, 'but it was only a woman.' 'I await you beyond time, where the snows are eternal,' she replies, 'but on this earth you must await and guide the other Ellis, who did not exist till you created her. Your voyage is near its end: but that is not the true end; for nothing ends save in God.' And tracing in the snow a text from Paul's Epistle to the Hebrews: 'And these received not the promise, to

[1] This prank was played upon Gide by Henri de Régnier during a visit to Belle-Isle, the island off Brittany, in August 1892, at the very time when Gide was writing this chapter of *Urien*. Gide was reading his Bible or *Wilhelm Meister* (at the time of telling the story, more than thirty years later, Régnier did not remember which), when Régnier threw one or the other into the water, enquiring: 'Gide, why are you reading this at the seaside?' But Gide, more pertinacious than poor Ellis, dived in to rescue his book.

[2] Cf. Wilde's epigram quoted above.

[3] This final section owes much to Jules Verne's *Captain Hatteras: or, The English at the North Pole*.

the end that they without us should not be made perfect,'[1] the
spiritual Ellis ascends to heaven and is acclaimed by the angels. A
little farther on they reach the Pole, beyond which is nothing but
an unfrozen lake and an ice-free sea. It is the end of the journey.
The companions kneel 'to await the return of the fidelity of
things', and Urien finishes with a confession to Ellis:

> Madam, I have deceived you:
> We have not made this voyage.
> We have not seen the gardens, nor
> The beaches' pink flamingos. . . .
> Temptations never came. . . .
> So I preferred to tell these lies[2], and still
> To wait, to wait, to wait.

Remy de Gourmont's prophecy had come true: Gide had awak-
ened armed with irony. In *Urien*, as in so many of Gide's works,
may be traced two main trends of significance, one universal, and
one personal. *Urien* is a satire on the spiritual quest, on action without living. The chaste voyagers resist temptation and find only
ennui; they reach the Pole, and can do nothing but kneel and wait
for life to catch up with them; and it is all as if they had never
been there. But the satire also attacks the symbolists and Parnas-
sians. Urien's epicene friends with the preposterous names are fit
only to embark on the Sargasso of Mallarmé's Tuesdays or the
fairy seas of Heredia's Saturdays; where some false knights would
retire into the inner drawing-room, whither Gide scorned to
follow, and chat, as to Haïatalnefus, with Mme Heredia and her
daughters.[3] But the most striking episode in *Urien* is that of the
two Ellises. The bookish Ellis is Gide-Walter's revenge upon a
Madeleine-Emmanuèle who has refused him and become an en-
cumbrance. The angelic Ellis is an affirmation of the survival of
their spiritual love: but his treatment of her, too, is not exempt
from irony.

[1] This text is quoted by Alissa in *Strait is the Gate* at her last meeting with
Jerome. In both cases, one suspects, Gide is repeating, for his cousin's eyes, words
that had passed between them in the 1880s.

[2] Cf., again, Wilde's epigram.

[3] Marie became the wife of Henri de Régnier in 1895, and Louise, temporarily,
of Pierre Louÿs in 1899.

In the summer of 1893 Gide attacked the subject from a new angle with a new 'treatise' – *La Tentative amoureuse, ou Traité du vain désir (The Attempt at Love: or, Treatise of Vain Desire)*. Rachel gives herself to Luc in the spring. All summer, in a château which is a portrait of La Roque, they enjoy the increasing boredom of love's pleasures, and in the autumn they part. 'Are you not all my life?' asks Rachel. 'But you are not all mine,' Luc answers, 'there are other things as well.' The opposition here is not between love and chastity, but between love and freedom. Gide was now approaching the opposite pole from his self-dedication to his cousin eleven years before. 'I shall taste the beauty I have denied myself,' he wrote in his journal, 'not as a sinner, in secret, with the bitter foretaste of repentance; but without remorse, with joy and power.'

As early as 1890, when Gide wandered by the Lake of Annecy in the lyrical frenzy of composing *André Walter*, he had cried out to an imaginary companion of his future travels; and he foresaw this friend not in Louÿs, but in Paul-Albert Laurens, son of a then famous painter, and a contemporary at the École Alsacienne. He spent much of the summer of 1893 with Laurens and his family at Yport, and in October the two young men set out on a momentous journey. Urien, at last, was to take a voyage in reality; and Gide left, as he tells us, his Bible at home behind him.

From the ship, as they entered the harbour of Tunis, they saw golden flying-fish, and on the shore a line of camels. They travelled south through the desert, and at Susa Gide fell ill. The doctor suspected tuberculosis.[1] They wintered at Biskra, and while Laurens went out to paint the oasis, followed by their boy servant Athman, laden with easel and canvases, Gide would sit, convalescent, on the terrace of the hotel or in the public garden, watching the brown children playing about him. The Algerian spring, with the retreat of his illness, brought a new birth, a severance from his puritan upbringing, and a recognition of the true nature of his desires. The two young men, tired of a long virginity, resolved to

---

[1] In November 1892 Gide had begun his military service, but was invalided out after a single week. Diagnosis: tuberculosis – the disease of which his father had died.

'normalize' themselves, and shared the barbaric favours of an Ouled Naïl girl named Meriem; but Gide's sense of duty in this act of hygiene was different from his friend's. In the arms of Meriem he was conscious that his true desires lay elsewhere: with the boy Ali he had known at Susa, or with the children of the hotel terrace. The sudden arrival of Gide's mother, alarmed by the news of his recent haemorrhage, put an end, for the time being, to these revels. In April Gide and Laurens returned via Syracuse and Rome; in May they reached Florence (where Gide met Wilde again), and separated. Gide went to Geneva to consult Dr Andreæ, a friend of Uncle Charles Gide, who persuaded him, correctly, that not his respiratory but his nervous system was at fault: a course of hydrotherapy at Champel and a winter in the mountains were indicated.

Gide was soon joined at Champel by Pierre Louÿs. Fired by the tale of Meriem, Louÿs hurried to Algeria and carried her off to Constantine. A month of her charms inspired him to complete the prose sapphics of his *Chansons de Bilitis*, and to send Gide a telegram reading: 'Athman insane, married, Ouled Naïls back from Chicago singing Ta-ra-ra-boom-de-ay with English accent.'

Not all Louÿs' jests were so innocent. He had outlived his usefulness as a teacher of form and objectivity, and his intimacy with Gide was becoming a mock-friendly bombardment of practical jokes, admirable in their wit, but pathological in their underlying desire to wound, rooted in jealousy and consciousness of inferiority. He would send Gide spiteful missives addressed to Monsieur Urien or Mlle Andrée Gide, and signed Jules Laforgue, Maeterlinck, or Emmanuèle. Or Gide would receive an unstamped letter, for which he would have to pay fifty centimes: inside he would find only a sheet of paper, inscribed, with Louÿs' exquisite calligraphy and violet ink: 'Price, fifty centimes. To be continued.' Back in Paris, Gide found the insignificant dilettantism of Louÿs everywhere. He was bursting with a new experience, and was horrified to find the literary salons unchanged. Such was his sense of alienation that he felt tempted to suicide: instead, he retired to spend the autumn at Neuchâtel in Switzerland and, in a hotel where on the dining-room wall hung two placards, reading, 'The Lord is my

Shepherd, I shall not want,' and 'Raspberry Lemonade,' and later in the snow-covered La Brévine in the Jura, he wrote *Paludes* (*Marshlands*).

Marshlands is about a man who is writing a book called '*Marshlands*'. On what subject? That, precisely, is the difficult question all his friends ask; and because his book is intended to have the same meaning for every reader, he gives each a different answer: 'for the only way of communicating the same thing to everyone is to modify it according to the peculiarities of each.' And even Gide himself says in his preface: 'Before explaining my book to others, I must wait for others to explain it to me.'

'*Marshlands*' then, is about Tityrus, who lives by a marsh like the river of ennui in *Urien*, in a dwelling where, like Gide at La Roque, he can fish out of his bedroom window. He feeds at first on widgeons – then, warned by the Church that this is a great sin, he tries mudworms (like the herons in *Urien*) and grows to enjoy them. For the horror of it is, Tityrus is contented; and his author's object is, by portraying contentment in a life of intolerable boredom, to inspire discontent in his audience. 'I don't wish to induce action,' he says, 'but to disengage freedom.' Further explanations follow thick and fast. '*Marshlands*' is the story of one who is unable to travel – it is about animals living in dark caves, who have lost their sight from ceasing to make use of it – it is the tale of the normal man, the third person singular, who lives in each of us, and survives when we die – its moral is, that each of us is shut in, but thinks himself out of doors. And when his hearers complain that the case of Tityrus is too particular, he retorts with a favourite maxim of Gide's: 'It is enough that there is the possibility of generalization – generalization itself is the task of the reader and the critic.'

The author's friends are not only his audience, but the target of his satire. Angèle, a literary lady whose remarks are always infuriatingly and sometimes penetratingly sensible, is the Ellis of *Urien*; but so extensively modified that she has lost all likeness to Gide's cousin. 'My great friend Hubert' is evidently Pierre Louÿs,[1]

---

[1] But he is also in part Gide's new friend Eugène Rouart, to whom his book, to the great annoyance of Louÿs, was dedicated.

as Louÿs himself recognized, when, after borrowing the MS. of *Marshlands* from Valéry, he wrote to Gide pretending he had destroyed it:

> 'My great friend Hubert'
> Did not burn *Marshlands.*
> In that point, at least,
> I differ from him.

He is a man of action: he rides, conducts charitable works and a company for insurance against hail, and on Sundays he hunts. Richard has some traits borrowed from Gide's cousin Albert Démarest. And Tancrède, author of the line 'Victorious captains smell abominably,' is Léon-Paul Fargue.

The author, after unsatisfactory interviews with all the characters, visits the Jardin des Plantes in search of data on the lesser potamogeton. That day he finds eight new epithets for the word blastoderm. He attends a literary evening at Angèle's, where his friends assail him with criticisms of his unwritten book, and he arranges that Angèle and he shall take a journey which will be the dawn of a new life, a shedding of monotony. That night he has horrible nightmares, in which the guests pursue him along endless corridors. He wakes at eight, crosses out the first item on his agenda,[1] which reads: 'Try to get up at six,' substitutes 'Get up at eleven,' and sleeps till noon. On the evening of their journey he dines with Angèle and sends her to sleep with an unlikely anecdote of a duckshoot in which his airgun 'made exactly the sound of "palm" in a line of Mallarmé.' Alas, their journey is a failure. It rains, and as they have unfortunately chosen a Saturday, they have to return in time for church next day. And then, a thunderbolt – Hubert leaves for Biskra! The author telegrams, 'Oh, Hubert, what of your charities?' and receives the reply, 'Balls, letter follows.' And the author begins to write a sequel to *Marshland* called *Netherlands.* That is all, except for a partly blank page in which the reader is requested to insert 'a table of the most remarkable phrases in *Marshlands.*'

[1] A parody of the lists of good resolutions of which Gide's *Journal* at this time is full.

Much of the fictional author's thought, it will be seen, is very near the truth. But if he is so successful in diagnosing the malady of his friends, it is because he is himself incurably infected with it. The writer of the imaginary '*Marshlands*' is a Tityrus who is able to be discontented, but unable to cease to be a Tityrus. Gide's book, the real *Marshlands*, is a work of Voltairean gaiety and superb style: Léon Blum, in those days a literary man, said: 'I thought nothing could be better written than *Marshlands*, until I read *Fruits of the Earth*.' In writing it Gide, by a typical stratagem, had inoculated himself against a disease and liberated himself for new health.

In January 1895 Gide set out again for Algeria. His two months' wintering at La Brévine in the Jura, where he slept with his window open to the freezing night, had restored his lungs, and now he longed for the North African spring. In a fit of daring he asked his mother to join him with Madeleine: the invitation was refused, but without rigour, for the idea of a match which might stabilize the wandering André was gaining ground in the family. Gide himself was convinced that with patience he would inevitably gain consent to his marriage.

Blidah was in the grip of an icy wind from the Atlas. Gide was preparing to leave when he saw on the list of visitors the names of Wilde and Lord Alfred Douglas. He erased his own name and left, then, ashamed of his cowardice, returned and re-registered. Wilde, Gide found, was much changed: some premonition that a breaking-point in his life lay close ahead had stripped him of reserve. That night he led Gide in search of 'Arab boys as beautiful as bronze statues': there were none to be found, but in Algiers, where he rejoined Gide some days later, matters were more efficiently organized. Gide's spiritual love, for the rest of his life, was dedicated to the chaste image of his cousin: his body ever after was to find its joy from the pleasures into which Wilde initiated him, a willing convert, in those few days in Algiers. Wilde left for England, there to be insulted by the 'terrible Marquess' and to meet the ruin he seemed half to desire: 'I have followed my own path as far as possible,' he had told Gide, 'I can go no farther – and now, *something else* is bound to happen.' The

something else was to be Reading Gaol. Gide left for Biskra
where, freed by his joy for a return of moral fervour, he began to
write *Fruits of the Earth*. He was recalled in March by urgent letters
from his anxious mother. Poor lady – her ruling urge had ever
been to insist on her own virtues in others; but her power over her
son had long waned. They spent a last fortnight together in
Paris, untroubled for once by quarrels; except that she tried in vain
to induce him to change the title of *Fruits of the Earth*, in which, no
doubt, the word 'earth' seemed to her suspect. When in May he
joinèd her at La Roque, she was dying, already unable to recognize her son. Her death gave him possession of the fortune she had
inherited from her father, and removed the last obstacle to his
marriage, to which, in any case, she had at last consented.

Mme Gide died on 31 May. On 17 June Gide and his cousin were
engaged. 'Dear André,' she wrote, 'am I not your friend, your
sister, your betrothed? *Sister* might perhaps seem quite absurd to
others – in my eyes it corresponds very well to what I am, and
what I feel.'

Neither bridegroom nor bride was normally fitted for normal
marriage. Gide was now a conscious homosexual, though still
unaware how totally so. Madeleine, permanently maimed by her
discovery in early adolescence of her mother's infidelity, had been
no less dominated by the memory of her gentle and wronged
father than André by the presence of his virile and self-righteous
mother. To André's continued appeals for their union she had replied again and again that she dreaded – 'with moral terror, an
ever increasing distaste' – marriage, 'so-called happiness', any
change in the form of their spiritual love. There were hints between them, and within the family, that this marriage of first
cousins might remain unconsummated. They had always called
each other brother and sister, and it is possible that each expected
and wished as husband and wife to be nothing more.

However, before this engagement Gide consulted an eminent
but unnamed neurologist, and made a total confession of his perversion. 'Marry without fear,' replied this reassuring imbecile
with a smilè, 'and you will soon realize that everything else exists
only in your imagination. You seem to me like a starving man

who has tried till now to feed on nothing but pickled gherkins.'[1]
Gide enquired also whether the children of a marriage between
first cousins would be defective, and received the same encourag-
ing reply. This second verdict may well have been as deluded as
the first, but was never to be put to the test.

[1] 'I quote his words exactly,' wrote Gide forty-five years after, 'damn it, I
remember them well enough.'

3

MARRIAGE

Fruits of the Earth, El Hadj, Saul, Prometheus Misbound:
Philoctetes, The Return, King Candaules

'No one takes a walk under palm-trees with impunity.' – LESSING (quoted in Gide's lecture, 'On Influence in Literature,' March 1900).

On 8 October 1895 Gide married his cousin Madeleine Rondeaux. The ceremony was performed at Étretat by the Protestant Pastor Roberty, who had conferred a similar service thirty-two years before on Gide's parents, and the best man was his former tutor, Pastor Élie Allégret. The young couple set out immediately for a long honeymoon. The autumn was spent at Neuchâtel ('I am beginning an indefatigable repose with the most tranquil of women,' Gide wrote to Francis Jammes[1]) and St. Moritz; the winter at Florence, Rome, and Naples; and in February, via Syracuse, they reached Tunis. Gide, seeking to reconcile past fervours with his married life, was following in reverse the route of his first return from Africa.

Their marriage, so it seems, was not consummated, then or ever. In Rome he took boy models to his room on the pretext of photographing them in the nude. In the train from Biskra to Algiers he flirted through the window with schoolboys in the next carriage. 'You looked like a criminal or a madman,' she admonished him afterwards. But despite these ominous incidents (which may in fact, as Jean Schlumberger has argued, have occurred only several years later), their strange honeymoon was a prelude to twenty years in which the moral intimacy of their early youth was re-

[1] Introduced by Eugène Rouart, they had been corresponding since May 1893, but had not yet met.

newed, deepened and prolonged. Gide's wife had replaced his
mother as a symbol of the pole of restraint and spiritual virtue to
which he needed always to be able to return, and without which
his other pole, of liberation, joy and perversion, would have lacked
all meaning.

In April they were joined by Eugène Rouart, bringing with him
Francis Jammes, vainest and most self-consciously limpid of minor
great poets. Gide saw 'a brisk little man with trumpet voice and
gimlet eyes,' Jammes a tall bearded youth with long hair, a cloak, a
Lavallière cravat, and 'the serene eyes of an ultra-modern Hugue-
not.' But to Gide's stupefaction Jammes soon took him aside and
said, 'We must take care not to say anything too subtle in Rouart's
presence'; and in a fortnight Jammes fled in jealous rage at seeing
Rouart's intelligence treated as equal with his own. However, he
was immensely taken with Athman, whom he taught to write
poetry. Athman did not care for Gide's *Attempt at Love*: 'You used
the word "grass" too often,' he said. And he wrote to Degas: 'What
I like about you is that, like me, you hate Jews and think Poussin a
great French painter.'

In May Gide returned to La Roque, and was immediately elec-
ted mayor of the district by a crushing majority. 'Those who maintain that I am indifferent to the public weal do not know the civic
zeal I brought to my very arduous functions,' he says, and piously
adds: 'Thank Heaven, France had reserved for her youngest mayor
one of her most minute communes.' He took his duties seriously,
joining young persons in matrimony and frightening alcoholics
into signing the pledge. He interested himself in Mulot, a dignified
labourer, whom he wished to make his constable – but the man had
been to prison, as he said, on an unjust charge of perjury. Gide
wished to have his case reopened ('I was at the age when injustice
causes an intolerable malaise, and in this respect I have aged little'[1]).
Long after he learned the truth – Mulot's crime had been the rape
of a little girl.

The rest of the year was spent at La Roque and at Cuverville
(which Gide's wife had inherited on the death of her father) in
the completion of *Les Nourritures terrestres (Fruits of the Earth)*,

[1] Written in *Jeunesse (Youth)*, a short autobiographical essay published in 1930.

begun during Gide's Tunisian convalescence in 1894, and published in April 1897. The *Fruits* relate the vision of truth from
which, in *Marshlands*, he had collected and jettisoned all that still
separated him. 'They are the harvest of my tuberculosis: it was the
epoch of my greatest fervours.'[1] And so, as befits the book of one
'who embraces life as a thing he has come near to losing,' the
Fruits are a hymn to the joy of life – or rather, to the life in which
everything is joy; to the pleasures of the senses – or rather,
to the state of being in which everything gives pleasure to the
senses.

The book is addressed to Nathanael, who has already made a
brief appearance as one of the companions of Urien. Unlike 'my
great friend Hubert', Nathanael had no existence in Gide's real
life. 'I have never met you,' he says, 'and I call you Nathanael, you
who one day will read me, because I do not know your future
name.' Gide's book is an arrow, and Nathanael is its target: he is
the ideal reader, he is you and I. Gide is already free: the object of
the book is to free Nathanael, without enrolling him as a disciple. 'Forget me. May my book teach you to feel interest more in
yourself than it – and then, in everything else more than in yourself.' And in Nathanael the sense of dissatisfaction which *Marshlands* ironically and deliberately failed to arouse, is taken for
granted. 'Nathanael, I will teach you fervour.'

The other chief character of the book is less imaginary. In the
course of his travels the author comes to Ménalque's villa, jutting
like the prow of an immense ship over Florence. Night-sounds of
the city rise like the faint murmur of waves, as Ménalque relates
his life to a mixed gathering which includes, naturally, Ydier,
Angaire, and other friends of Urien; surprisingly, several women,
Cléodalise, Simiane, and so on; and impossibly, Nathanael himself. Ménalque is Wilde, whom, as we have seen, Gide had met on
this very hill of Florence in 1894, and he is the Des Esseintes of
Huysmans. But he is also, like Walter, Urien, Tityrus (there were
to be many more) a discarded self of Gide, a wraith who, by
going too far in the direction of the book, has left the real Gide
free. So the extreme utterance of the author's doctrines is given to

---

[1] 2 July 1907. Letter to Christian Beck.

Ménalque: 'I hated the family, the home, all places where men think they can find rest. . . . Each new thing must find us always and utterly unattached. . . . Families, I hate you.' Ménalque has sold all his goods – an apostle could do no more. But with the proceeds he has bought the vast villa where he entertains his friends, and his only freedom will be to buy another villa somewhere else. He is, if not a *reductio ad absurdum*, a limiting case of the book's philosophy. And when dawn comes, the author, more truly 'unattached' than Ménalque, sets out again on his travels.

From every place Gide had visited on his two journeys, but above all from Tunisia, sensual joys flock to the *Fruits*. Sensual joy! – the very sound is abhorrent to puritans of every kind. In it the moral puritan shuns the flesh, the religious puritan suspects mysticism, the social puritan sees danger to society's foundations in the family and work for daily bread. And, most horrible, may not these joys be, as some have inferred, Gide's camouflage of sexual pleasure, in fact, of sexual deviation? If so, proof must be sought elsewhere, for the actual words of the *Fruits* will bear no such interpretation. Undoubtedly, one of the causes of Gide's explosive liberation was his discovery of sexual pleasure, but an equal cause was his discovery of travel. Sensual love is a powerful symbol of the body's freedom and the spirit's; but so also is the ability to wander. The prisoner in his cell wants love, but he also wants to walk about outside; ostensibly at least, the joys of love appear only shyly and rarely in the *Fruits*.

If we examine the pleasures Gide praises, we shall be struck most of all by their innocence. They soar through smell, hearing, touch, and sight to their crescendo in taste; from fruits, wheat-grains, and other vegetarian foods to the satisfactions of thirst; and the greatest of these is plain water!

> The sweetest joys of my senses
> Have been thirsts I have quenched.

And with the mystic joys of fasting and mere existence, his fervour is volatilized to its highest intensity: 'No wine gave me the vertigo of this abstinence' – '*Being* became infinitely voluptuous.' Gide's hedonism evolves into an asceticism. In the infinite catalogue of pleasures not one is presented literally and carnally: all are means whose end is spiritual liberation. 'Matter is infinitely porous to spirit.'

The *Fruits* are an attempt to make spiritual joy less sterile, less a mortification, by joining the body to it, by approaching it through the body. In this way, since the body's needs are inexhaustible, spiritual joy, it is hoped, may be made inexhaustible also. This formula for the conquest of the spirit closely approaches Rimbaud's 'reasoned derangement of all the senses' – but it is rather a reasoned *attention* of the senses that Gide sings. He had re-read Rimbaud at Coire in August 1894. 'He was my only viaticum in the most important months of convalescence of my whole life.' The ardour of *Fruits* is that of the *Illuminations,* the route is that of '*Bateau Ivre*': escape from towropes, a joyful course over the open sea, a succession of hallucinatory visions, and a partial capitulation, an admission of the brevity of joy, the claims of others. Gide finishes in Paris, regretting the desert: 'Anguish of thought. Others – the importance of *their* life – I must speak to them.' The state of joy to which the *Fruits* show the way has led not to exaltation of the ego, but to depersonalization. 'Have you noticed that in this book there is No One? Even I am nothing in it but Vision.'

In his final state of simplicity and denudation, Nathanael will cease to feel interest in himself. He will be able to press on, for his desires will cease to call him back: he will be able to 'love his neighbour' without ulterior motive; he will, at last, be very close to God; for God waits on the far side of our desires, and to find him we must face and pass through them. 'Understand that at every instant of the day you can possess God wholly.' But all this is in the future, and will take place only when Nathanael has obeyed Gide's command and 'thrown away this book.' Salvation is always tomorrow: Gide has shown us not what we must do to be saved, but what we must do before we can be saved. In the final hymn he gives the word to his wife: she points to the stars, each by a free act of choice following the path traced for it by unalterable law, and says: 'We cannot save *ourselves.*'

In ten years, only five hundred copies of *Fruits of the Earth* were

Athman, aged 14, in 1893 (*Collection Mme Catherine Lambert Gide*)

Gide at Biskra, 1893 (*Bibliothèque Nationale*)

Meriem, aged 16, in the street of the Ouled Naïl at Biskra, 1893 (*Collection Mme Catherine Lambert Gide*)

Oscar Wilde, "to my dear friend André Gide, Dec. '91." (*Collection Mme Catherine Lambert Gide*)

sold. At the office of the *Mercure de France* it became a traditional jest to say to visitors: 'Won't you take a few *Fruits* away with you? There are plenty there, and they won't keep much longer.' It was not till the 1920s that Nathanael began to read Gide's book. And the *Fruits* brought a final break with Pierre Louÿs, who called its innocent Roundel of the Pomegranate 'a bomb-shell of filth and fornication'. In 1897 Louÿs wrote, in an obscene and witty satire, how Wilde and Montesquiou (the future Charlus of Proust) watched

> The entrance of a man whose soul was vile
> Gide, lord of La Roque and Cuckooverville,
> Whose hair is longer than a whoreless day,
> And on whose finger shines the morning star.

'There is not a phrase of your book that does not carry with it its own refutation,' Jammes wrote to Gide, seizing unawares on one of the cardinal points of Gide's moral and aesthetic philosophy. For the next ten years, until the completion of *Strait is the Gate,* Gide's works were to test the doctrine of *Fruits,* to point out its dangers, examine arguments for the other side, and elaborate on the text: 'Throw away this book.' There is perhaps no more convincing proof of that doctrine's truth, than the strength and perpetuity of the need to refute it. In *El Hadj,* written in the midst[1] of the creation of *Fruits,* Gide told of an invisible prince[2] who led his people through the desert of faith to the salt-pan shores of eternity, and a poet who led them back to their earthly city and, because they hailed him a prophet, knew he was none. So, for a moment, Gide saw his summons to joy as a retreat, and himself as a false prophet. But this, he found, was the least of the attacks he could launch against his own teachings.

On the publication of his book in April 1897 Gide, as was his custom, disappeared from Paris. He revisited Italy ('Ménalque has unfolded Italy before him,' he wrote to Jammes) and, anxious for his wife's health, ailing since their honeymoon, took her to Losdorf

---

[1] August 1896.

[2] The prince is Christ, and the poet Gide, viewing himself for the moment with irony and scorn.

in Switzerland for sulphur baths. In the summer he was at La Roque, writing *Saul,* and, in October, *Le Promethée mal enchaîné (Prometheus Misbound).* 'I admire, adore, venerate Madeleine,' he wrote to Jammes, 'her sweetness is incomparable, and, frail as she is, she is able to protect.' In the early spring of 1898 came a new journey, again in search of health for his wife, to Algeria. On the way home through Italy he completed *Prometheus,* and at Arco in the Tyrol he finished *Saul.*

The way through the *Fruits* had led to God, but via a Vale Perilous, where devils lay in wait for the sensual loiterer. It was in 'a crisis of pessimism, wounded pride, and contempt'[1] that Gide wrote 'as a counterpoise and antidote to *Fruits,*'[2] 'the terrible drama of King Saul.'[3] Its subject is 'the portrayal of that ruin of the soul, that bankruptcy and annihilation of personality, which is brought on by non-resistance to temptation.'[4] Saul, wishing to be the only prophet in Israel, has destroyed his rivals, and freed against himself all the demons that inhabited them. The demons are his own desires. One takes his crown, the others his purple robe, his wine-cup, his throne; the king is disintegrated. 'My value is in my complexity,' he says pathetically. His temptations are the apparently innocent joys of the *Fruits:* 'The least sound, the faintest perfume takes possession of me: my senses are open to the outside world, and no sweet thing passes unperceived by me.' And it is with hideous irony that his devils offer him the approach of dawn, grass soaked in dew, baths, an aniseed sherbet – pleasures already met in the *Fruits,* where they seemed so fair, here so treacherous. 'Everything that delights thee is thine enemy,' the witch of Endor tells him; and in his final state of Lear-like imbecility he says of his demon-desires, 'They have suppressed me completely.'

The direst of Saul's secrets is that he feels for David, the delightful enemy who will take his throne, a love that dares not speak its name. Saul slays his wife when she is on the point of discovering this. David, too, finds out, and it is the beginning of Saul's madness

[1] Letter to Raymond Bonheur, 8 September 1898.
[2] Letter to Pastor Ferrari, 15 March 1928.
[3] Letter to Jammes, July 1897.
[4] Letter to Father Poucel, 27 November 1928.

and the end of David's loyalty. Yet David's revulsion is not so much from the king's hidden lust, as from his own hidden acquiescence. His epitaph on the slaughtered tyrant is: 'I did not detest thee, King Saul.' Both David and Saul have something of Gide himself. Saul is Gide-Ménalque, demoralized by a lifetime of slavery to his own desires, and David, the serious youth for whom his parents had a pet-name which no others, save Jonathan, may use, is Gide-Walter. But in appearance David is modelled upon the bronzes of Donatello and Verrocchio, seen on the honeymoon visit to Florence; and like Athman,[1] he is a shepherd and a musician. He is the first appearance in Gide's works of a new ideal, that of the free stripling, dangerous in action, innocent because remorseless; he will culminate in the Lafcadio of *The Vatican Swindle* and the Bernard of *The Coiners*.

One could almost, Gide may have felt, forgive a doom that came from a David; and perhaps, if David had been more free . . . for David claims to be only the instrument of the Lord. Certainly, Saul's punishment is too drastic to be a mere natural consequence of his actions, and suggests a hostile intervention from above – *quem Deus vult perdere, prius dementat.* Saul is a great man who, in his non-resistance to temptation, is only obeying the precepts of *Fruits of the Earth* – what if he had, in the English army phrase, 'refused to accept his punishment'? In the Bible there was a moral bias with which Gide found his Protestant self agreeing too easily. In future, when he required a mythological subject, he turned not to the Hebrews but to the Greeks. Even before the completion of *Saul*, the antidote to the *Fruits*, Gide had written *Prometheus Misbound*, which is an antidote to *Saul*.

In Greek legend the ideal of a great man unjustly punished by heaven was found in Prometheus, whom Zeus chained to the Caucasus, sending an eagle daily to feed on his liver, because he tried to make men free. But Gide's Prometheus, finding that his chains 'and other scruples' give him cramp, gets up and walks away. He descends the boulevard leading from the Madeleine to the Opéra, and sits down in a restaurant where he is joined by

[1] Athman had told Gide Arab legends of David, calling him Daoud, which Gide makes David's pet-name. See *'Feuilles de route'* in *Amyntas*.

Damocles and Cocles, both in a state of acute anxiety. Damocles
has received, in an envelope addressed in an unknown hand (whose
only characteristics, graphologists tell him, are good nature and
weakness), a five-hundred-franc note. Where can he find his bene-
factor? And Cocles has restored a dropped handkerchief to a stout
gentleman, who, after requesting him to write any address he
chose on an envelope, gave him a violent slap on the face. On the
envelope received by Damocles, Cocles recognizes his own hand-
writing. He raises his hand to slap the cause of his woes, but is
prevented by the waiter. It is time to change the subject. Surely,
they ask, Prometheus, too, has some distinctive trait? He confesses
shyly to his eagle, and is asked to show it. He calls, and the eagle
flies in, smashing the window, dashing out Cocles' eye, and resumes his meal on the liver of Prometheus.

Cocles is delighted with his new glass eye, Damocles falls ill
through worrying what to do with the five hundred francs,
Prometheus feeds his eagle till it becomes sleek and beautiful. He
invites the public to a lecture. The subject is: Eagles. Prometheus
used to love his fellow-men, but now he only loves what devours
them – their eagles. An eagle is a man's individuality, the virtue or
vice, duty or passion in which he differs from other men, his reason
for existence. Cocles' eagle is his slap on the face, Damocles' is his
five hundred francs. A famished eagle is a mere conscience. Every
man must feed his eagle; his recompense will be to see it grow into
beauty.

Prometheus and the waiter call on Zeus the millionaire, the
dealer of slaps and banknotes, and beg him to visit Damocles, who
is dying because he does not know to whom he owes his own good
fortune and Cocles' disaster. Zeus refuses – 'I should lose my
prestige,' he says. Prometheus asks to see Zeus's eagle. 'I don't keep
eagles,' Zeus laughs, 'I give them to others.' 'Some people say you
are God almighty,' suggests the waiter, and Zeus does not deny it.

In the pleasant discourse that Prometheus pronounces over the
grave of Damocles, we meet some old friends. Tityrus (Gide) lives
in the midst of marshes (La Roque), till Ménalque (Wilde) passes
by, and plants an idea in the mind of Tityrus and an acorn in his
marshland. Round the vast oak springs up a vast community, of

which Tityrus (like Gide of La Roque) is made mayor. His joy has become a duty – Angèle persuades him to leave it, and in turn leaves him, and Tityrus finds himself again surrounded by marshes.

It remains only for Prometheus to invite Cocles to dinner in their old restaurant. Their delicious meal is the eagle of Prometheus! 'It ate me long enough,' he explains, 'and I decided it was my turn.' 'Then nothing remains of all its beauty,' sighs Cocles. 'I have kept its feathers,' Prometheus replies. 'And from one of them,' Gide adds confidentially, 'I made the pen with which I wrote this book.'

Prometheus, like *Marshlands,* was written in the autumn following a summer visit to Paris. Gide in Paris was surrounded by literary rivals who were his inferiors. The price they demanded for admiring his works was one that he could not pay: that he in return should admire theirs. Gide was not to feel at home in Paris literary circles until, in the next decade, a new generation of young disciples had grown up around him. His satire in *Marshlands* and *Prometheus* has a brilliant gaiety that comes of exasperation partly digested, and partly turned against himself. But the meaning of *Prometheus* is more serious than its manner. It is a re-justification and an extension of *Fruits*: the quest for individual value, discouraged in *Saul*, is again obligatory. Virtue and vice, passion and duty are, in this aspect, of equal worth; and when the quest is completed, its result can itself be abandoned and utilized; we may eat our eagle. And the jealous God of Saul is put in his place: for Jehovah is also Zeus, the irresponsible dealer of undeserved slaps and financial windfalls; and, here at any rate, he is subordinated to the gay, euphoric figure of man as Hero.

The figure of the hero, but re-associated now with renunciation and 'denudation', reappears in *Philoctetes,* begun in 1894 simultaneously with *Marshlands* and *Fruits,* and finished at La Roque in the autumn of 1898. *Philoctetes* is in the form of a play, but Gide expressly states that it is not meant for performance, and, under the sub-title 'Treatise of the Three Moralities', classes it among his treatises. Ulysses and Neoptolemus have come to Philoctetes' ice-bound island to steal his bow, which alone can give the Greeks victory at Troy. In the unscrupulous nationalist morality of Ulysses there is an evident reference to the Dreyfus affair, now at its height; Gide, of course, was an ardent Dreyfusard.[1] Neoptolemus is the innocent and dangerous boy David again. Philoctetes, obeying a devotion to something higher than the gods or patriotism ('To what?' asks Neoptolemus, and 'To oneself,' he stammers), gives up the bow, his last possession, and is rewarded with the utter happiness of utter destitution.

Two more works, both commenced at La Roque in July 1899, closed Gide's cycle of dramatic production. *Le Retour (The Return)* is an accomplished and charming verse libretto for a projected domestic opera by Raymond Bonheur. Horace is a husband who returns from three happy years of toil in a tropical country to the wife with whom, before their marriage, his childhood was spent. 'How small the room is,' he exclaims, and his wife says, 'But when we were children, in the evening, it seemed huge.' And Marthe's younger sister Lucille is evidently in love with Horace, just as Madeleine's sister Valentine Rondeaux had for a time been in love with Gide. Gide completed only the first act, seeing no doubt that the plot encroached prematurely not only on his private life, but on the themes of his future novels, *The Immoralist* and *Strait is the Gate*.

In *Le Roi Candaule (King Candaules)*, his last play till *Oedipus* in 1931, Gide uses the legend from Herodotus of the Lydian king who, overproud of his wife's beauty, displayed her naked to his humble subject, Gyges. Gyges then slew his master and became king himself. Gide makes of Candaules a special case of the philosophy of *Fruits* – a man who is unable to feel the full immensity of his happiness unless he shares it with others. Or so he alleges in his preface; but he cannot have been unaware that the voluntary sharing of one's wife, whatever its metaphysical implications, is also a well-known form of sexual perversion. Later[2] he was pleased to find himself anticipated by Dostoevsky (Mysh-

---

[1] Francis Jammes in fact mentions in his autobiography that the Dreyfus Case was fervently discussed at La Roque every morning from 10 o'clock till lunch, during his visit in September 1898.

[2] *Journal*, 2 December 1905.

kin's surrender of Nastasya to Rogozhin in *The Idiot*), but later still[1] he called *Candaules* 'the least important of my works.' It is certainly the least individual, except in so far as it is a rehash of *Saul*. But it was far from deserving its reception. Gide had the amusing idea, 'in order to assist the reader in forming an opinion, if he wishes to have one,' of prefacing the second edition of *Candaules* (1904) with a little garland of criticisms culled from the newspapers. Their oafish illiteracy is quite astonishing, and nothing, in our days of educated critics and no literature, could more strikingly explain the smallness of Gide's audience during his first twenty years as a writer. 'I couldn't understand a word,' said *Le Figaro* and eleven others. 'It is subtle,' the *Semaine Française* complained, while Gaston Leroux, the writer of detective stories, felt that 'a work of such simplicity could be a masterpiece in intention only.' But the eminent Faguet weighed in with a glowing tribute: 'M. André Gide's play is by no means clumsily put together, and there is a certain agreeableness in its style.'

[1] Letter to Maurras in *Journal*, 20 October 1916.

4

INQUIETUDE, INFLUENCE AND CONSTRAINT

The Immoralist, In Memoriam: Oscar Wilde, Pretexts, Amyntas

'In the Normandy autumn I dream of the desert spring.' – *Amyntas*.

It might have seemed that the possibilities of *Fruits* had now been fully examined and exhausted; yet one, and the most important, still remained. In prose-poem, drama, and satire Gide had kept the problems of self-realization always at one remove – it remained to show them at work no longer in fantasy, but in their actual terror and beauty, as they would appear in real life, and as Gide himself had wrestled with them during the past seven years. Is it in fact possible to *live* according to the philosophy of *Fruits,* and what are the consequences of the attempt on oneself, one's fellow-creatures, and in particular one's wife? To answer these questions a novel was required, and Gide wrote *The Immoralist.*[1]

To please his dying father, Michel, a puritanical young scholar, marries Marceline, who is, like himself, innocent and orphan. His acquiescence in a loveless marriage is quickly punished. No sooner have they reached North Africa on their honeymoon than he falls gravely ill, has a haemorrhage, and accepts the idea of death. Marceline nurses him devotedly but unskilfully, and a second haemorrhage retards his convalescence, just as he begins to see the

---

[1] First conceived at Biskra in 1894, later intended as a 'Life of Ménalque', commenced probably in October 1900, finished 25th October 1901, published in May 1902.

potential beauty of the life he is in danger of leaving. 'I want life, I want to live,' he cries, and henceforth takes charge of his own cure – it is the first of many acts of will. Health, he decides, is good, and anything that does not conduce to health is evil.

Michel returns again to life, this time by his own efforts. They are at Biskra, and spring is beginning. He ventures into the public gardens, then as his strength increases, explores the whole oasis. Marceline introduces him to some Arab children, and Michel gets to know more on his own account. His wife prefers those who are good and ailing, Michel prefers the others, and most of all one whom he watches stealing his wife's scissors. This miniature crime fills Michel with joy, no doubt because he too has robbed Marceline – but the scene is full also of a more Freudian symbolism.

They return home via Syracuse and Italy. On the road to Sorrento Michel has a fight with a drunken carriage-driver,[1] and that night, for the first time, he consummates his marriage. He feels love for Marceline, but more pity than love; he realizes that he has become stronger than she. They enter a period of short-lived calm and joy, and at La Morinière, Michel's country house in Normandy, Marceline finds she is pregnant. Michel interests himself in the work of his farm, in riding, and in Charles, son of his steward.

They spend the winter in Paris, where Michel is disgusted by the lack of individuality of everyone he meets. 'But you cannot expect everyone to differ from everyone else,' says Marceline. In Ménalque Michel meets one who demands precisely that. Ménalque has been to Biskra, and hands Michel the stolen scissors, which prove that Michel, at least, differs from others; for the boy Moktir has told Ménalque all. Michel leaves the sick Marceline in order to spend the last night of Ménalque's sojourn in Paris in a final conversation. 'One must choose,' says Ménalque, 'but the important thing is to know what one wants' – and he advises Michel to keep his 'calm happiness.' When Michel returns home next morning he finds his wife has had a miscarriage and is dangerously ill. It is Michel's turn to nurse her.

[1] Gide had a similar experience with a runaway carriage and a drunken driver in Brittany, alone, in 1889.

Marceline seems to recover, and they return to La Morinière. Michel becomes more engrossed in his farm workers than in his farm. Displeased by Charles, now a gentleman with side-whiskers, he joins the local bad boys in poaching his own game. Charles finds him out, and Michel, annoyed and embarrassed, announces that he is selling La Morinière. 'Let us travel again,' he tells Marceline, 'and you will find that I still love you as I did at Sorrento.'

Their second honeymoon follows the route of their first in reverse. Michel persuades himself that Marceline needs the warm south; but in reality he is seeking a renewal for himself of his re-birth in Tunisia. 'What she called happiness I called rest, and I did not want to rest.' 'I understand your doctrine,' Marceline tells him. 'It is beautiful, perhaps, but it suppresses the weak.'[1] He drags his dying wife ever southwards; they reach Touggourt, and she dies of the tuberculosis she had contracted in nursing him. Michel sends for his friends to hear his story and give him help. 'I want to live,' he had cried two years before, and now he says, 'Take me away and give me some reasons for existing.' 'I have searched for my individual value, and found it consists in an obstinate pursuit of the worst,' he confesses. But he is impenitent: 'I feel nothing in myself that is not noble.'

To what extent is *The Immoralist* the story of Gide's own marriage? The parallels are very close, but very deceptive. The route, illness, recovery, and initiation of Michel's first journey come not from Gide's own honeymoon, but from the North African trip with Paul Laurens in 1893–4, two years before Gide's marriage. Gide's actual calmer and happier honeymoon in 1895–6 resembled the desperate race towards death of Michel's second journey in route only. In real life Madeleine Gide never had to nurse her husband in a dangerous illness; it was he, on the contrary, who devotedly nursed her. Their trips to Switzerland in May 1897 and to Algeria in spring 1898, both in search of health for Madeleine have already been mentioned. In August 1898 came more sulphur baths at Losdorf, and in the spring of 1899 they had

---

[1] The opposite of Saul's saying of his demon-desires 'They have suppressed me completely.'

to hurry home from another visit to Tunisia – 'our exhausted wills could prolong no more the agony of this journey.'[1] In July 1900 Madeleine Gide broke both arms in a carriage accident, and with her recovery from this mishap her general health seems to have improved. She resembled Marceline in goodness and innocence, but not in fate.

Gide's journal, in these crucial years from 1896 to 1901 is not available;[2] but from retrospective entries in the resumed journal of 1902 and from the letters may be gathered several hints for the figure of Michel. The dread word 'inquietude', Gidian for 'Angst', appears more and more frequently, and will dominate the next decade. Gide suffered for a time from his nerves, and in the October of 1899 and 1900 went alone to Lamalou, in Provence, to recuperate. 'I think something in my life is about to change,' he· wrote thence to Jammes, 'I feel like a clock on the point of striking.'[3] In 1900 and 1901 he developed an obsession – this is very like Michel – for night-prowling on the boulevards,[4] which he partly cast off after *The Immoralist* was written. And in the summer of 1900 came an incident that seems like some chapter of *The Immoralist*, rejected because stranger than fiction. In 1895 he had proposed to bring Athman to Paris, but was prevented by the horror of his mother, and her old servant Marie, who said, 'If that Negro comes, I go.' But now his new accomplice Henri Ghéon escorted the Arab youth from North Africa, and together with Gide they frequented the Tunisian quarter of the Universal Exposition, where J. E. Blanche painted them, sitting in a mock native café with Eugène Rouart and Chanvin. Ghéon liked to trace a growing cynicism in Blanche from this date! Michel's La Morinière is of course, Gide's La Roque; and in 1900 Gide, like Michel, put this, his mother's home, up for sale. He visited it occasionally on business, but was never to live there again.

Once more Gide had written a work which portrayed not so

[1] Letter to Jammes, April 1899.

[2] We do not know whether it was unwritten, destroyed with pre–1890 diaries in 1902 or later, or suppressed.

[3] Letter to Jammes, October 1900. He had taken baths at Lamalou after his hysterical seizure in 1881.

[4] *Journal* for 8 January 1902 and May 1905.

much his own state of mind, as a danger from which he wished, by describing it, to save himself. He wrote it 'in sweat and tears,' 'lived it for four years and wrote it in order to pass beyond'; 'if I had not written my *Immoralist* I risked becoming him.'[1] In real life Gide, or a transitory part of him, was Michel, but without Michel's crimes. He was able to seek joy without final spiritual disintegration, and without killing his wife.

The Immoralist is a cautionary tale of a cruel individualist; but it is too nearly, also, his glorification. Gide, most readers will feel, does not sufficiently condemn his villainous hero; he even shows him an oblique complaisance. Michel's final unhappiness is not enough to counterbalance his virtual murder of wife and child, and he lacks, being insufficiently punished, the saving pathos of Saul and Candaules, who are punished too much. As is always the case when a work of art chooses to set an ethical problem with bias and leaves it unresolved, the moral flaw is felt as an aesthetic flaw.

If *The Immoralist* is immediately recognizable as a masterpiece, it is not for its sinister depths, but for its delightful surface. Gide never wasted effort on making his works difficult to enjoy. In *The Immoralist* his narrative reaches an ease and charm, his prose a limpid perfection, which he had previously only hinted, and then with irony, in his satires. These qualities he was to vary infinitely in mood and complexity, but rarely, perhaps never to surpass. But the chief impressions that we carry away from *The Immoralist,* apart from the ugly memory of Michel, are the joys of Gide's own life in the 1890s: the idyll of convalescence at Biskra, the georgic of La Morinière, the eclogue of Ménalque's conversation. These episodes owe something of their ideal beauty to the fact that they are also elegies: on the oases of Tunisia to which Gide's next visit was to be a farewell, on the woods and waters of La Roque abandoned to the steward, on the gilded voice of Wilde now stilled for ever. Gide's good-bye has perpetuated them.

Wilde had died in December 1900, and Gide had heard the news at Biskra with his wife, too far away to follow the ill-attended hearse to the grave in Père Lachaise. Instead, a year later, as soon

[1] Letters to Jammes.

as he was freed from the novel of Ménalque and his disciple, he wrote *In Memoriam: Oscar Wilde*. Scandal, prison, and death had exercised a curious pejorative effect on critical opinion of Wilde's works, and Gide himself admired him more as a living force and example than as a writer.[1] 'Why aren't your plays better?' he had asked Wilde reproachfully at Algiers. 'Why do you talk the best in yourself, instead of writing it?' And Wilde had replied: 'I have put my genius into my life, I have put only my talent into my works.'

Probably for every English reader of Gide's essay, a hundred more have learned from Boris Brasol's and Hesketh Pearson's biographies of Wilde, that R. H. Sherard wrote a pamphlet called *Oscar Wilde Twice Defended against André Gide's Wicked Lies,* and that Mr Brasol and Mr Pearson endorse his views. Sherard, like so many of Wilde's friends, believed himself the only real friend Wilde ever had. His pamphlet, despite its genuine indignation and execrable prose, fails to prove either inaccuracy or malice in Gide's account of Wilde. Instead, Gide's wreath on an abandoned tomb, as he called it, is by far the most convincing and sympathetic account we have of Wilde's conversation and presence, of the genius he devoted not to writing but to living.[2] The Wilde of *In Memoriam,* like the Ménalque of *Fruits* and *The Immoralist,* is an oddly serious Wilde, without his art and without his epigrams; but this is precisely the Wilde that Gide saw, and who would otherwise be lost to us. In his conversations with Gide, Wilde rarely dared or cared to utter an epigram, and when he did was immediately told off for frivolity. Wilde reserved his wit for those he wished to amuse or annoy. With Gide he felt that his soul was on trial; it is very likely that Gide helped him to acquire one, and that we owe a little of *De Profundis* to Gide just as we owe something of *Fruits of the Earth* to Wilde.

In 1903 Gide republished the study of Wilde in *Pretexts,* together

[1] 'Certainly, in my little book on Wilde, I was hardly fair towards his work, and dismissed it too lightly. I mean without having got to know it well enough." – *Journal,* 29 June 1913.

[2] Wilde's friend Robert Ross told Gide that *In Memoriam* was 'not only the best account of Oscar Wilde at the different stages of his career, but the only true and accurate impression of him that I have ever read'.

with essays and reviews from *L'Ermitage,* and the 'Letters to
Angèle' from the *Mercure de France.* In the spring of 1898 the
Angèle of *Marshlands* had insisted on breaking into *Prometheus
Misbound,* and for the following two years Gide had amused himself with writing rude, witty letters to this literary lady. She is a
surprisingly living figure. I have suggested that she stems from
Urien's Ellis,[1] but cannot help suspecting some lost original among
the lady manageresses of literary salons whom Gide had frequented
in the early '90s. When a certain Mme Brandon appals her guests
by saying to Gide as he leaves, 'Persons with whom one finds
pleasure in talking are so rare'[2] one hears a dying fall of the
Angèle of *Marshlands.* These letters (except for a few epistles
in 1921) are the last appearance of Angèle. With her Gide abandoned irony for ten years, until *The Vatican Swindle.*

Much of the literature handled in *Pretexts* is now for ever forgotten, but Gide's criticism, being superior to its victims, survives,
calling to mind Wilde's paradox, a favourite with Gide: 'The
imagination can only imitate; it is criticism that creates.' These
essays and reviews are more than burnings, by a masterly public
hangman, of bad books, more than manœuvres in a literary civil
war. They are, in fact, 'pretexts' for the free play of Gide's mind.
The critic Souday of *Le Temps,* a lover of milk and water,
preferred Gide's criticism above all his works. Possibly, if he had
realized its dangerous originality, the quantity of brandy in the
milk, he would have damned it faintly with the rest. Yet the
underlying trend of *Pretexts* is already one of retreat from Gide's
extreme position of the 1890s. Freedom, 'uprootedness', individualism are now the prerogative and burden of genius; the
weak and ordinary had better remain planted where they are. 'I
distrust the failures of individualism,' he tells Angèle, 'just as much
as any other failures. The greater the individuals, the fewer. If
everyone were an individual, individuals would cease to exist. For

---

[1] Written in 1950. In the posthumous *Et Nunc Manet in Te* (1951) Gide remarks
that he depicted his wife as Emmanuèle in *Les Cahiers d'André Walter* and as Ellis in
Le Voyage d'Urien, and that 'even in the evanescent Angèle of *Paludes* I took my
inspiration in some small degree from her.'

[2] *Journal,* 26 January 1908. Mme Brandon was a friend of Gide's mother, and
her salon was the first he attended in his youth.

the love of the Self, let's have no more individualism!' And describing to Angèle the last state of Nietzsche, happy, but no longer remembering his own name, he says: 'Au revoir, my dear – may God measure out your happiness in small doses!'

The lecture, 'On Influence in Literature', which opens *Pretexts* marks a stage of even more capital importance in Gide's development. Paradoxically, this individualist scolds his contemporaries for their dread of undergoing influence, for a desire to be original at all costs, that implies an unacknowledged doubt of their own originality. Influence, he says, is not an imposition of an alien personality, but a means of discovering one's own – it is an explanation of oneself. Gide, as we learn from countless entries in his journal, was beginning to read again; he was courting influences. His first springtime of *Fruits* was coming to an end; he could not foresee what should come next, and set out to explore and cultivate his unexploited powers. His re-readings of Stendhal in 1902 and 1905, of Dostoevsky in 1903, of Mérimée in 1904, of Rimbaud and Lautréamont in 1905, were not mere exercises in blood-transfusion. The gaiety, pride, and subtlety of Stendhal, Dostoevsky's deep-mining into evil and redemption, the exquisite storytelling of Mérimée, were already latent in Gide; in these writers he found not a bankrupt's subsidies, but 'explanations of himself.' He might have remained a Nietzschean neo-symbolist for ever; he was to become, though in ways entirely characteristic of himself, a Stendhal, a Dostoevsky, and finally a Goethe.

The next ten years after *The Immoralist,* up to the commencement of *The Vatican Swindle* in 1911, were the least productive of Gide's early maturity. His trajectory from the explosive revelation at Biskra in 1893 had reached its downward slope, and he had entered a period of transition and preparation. He was growing a new skin under cover of the old, or rather, like a chrysalis, he was preparing for a metamorphosis. The transition is visible in the few works of this decade, in *Amyntas, The Return of the Prodigal Son, Strait is the Gate, Isabelle,* only because they bid farewell to the past. They contain no hint of the future. Consciously or unconsciously, he was not advancing, but exhausting and amassing possibilities. At times he was hampered by a terrible sense of urgency: 'In order to be what I am, I have not a moment to lose.'

His other 'influences' were of a more practical order. As he had promised in *Fruits of the Earth,* he was becoming interested 'in others, the importance of *their* life – I must speak to them.' In 1905, for the first of many times, he chose a Nathanael in his young cousin Paul Gide, and helped him to freedom. He welcomed a new generation of friends; not would-be mentors like Louÿs and Régnier, nor mighty opposites like Valéry and Claudel (Jammes was a middle-sized opposite), but men younger than himself, who came to him for love of his works. Ghéon, Copeau, Schlumberger, Jaloux, Rivière had, for the time being, no desire to alter him. They might disobey him by refraining from 'throwing away his book', but they did not use his book as an indictment against him. And he followed the old ambivalent impulse that, even in his schooldays, had made him wish to launch a literary review and then disappear from it. He entered with his friends into *L'Ermitage,* and from 1903 sat on the editorial committee with Remy de Gourmont. He was called the 'Grey Eminence' of the review. *L'Ermitage* died in 1906, and in 1909 he helped with organization and money to found the *Nouvelle Revue Française.* Yet here, too, he remained in the background, and only the names of Copeau, Schlumberger, and André Ruyters appeared on the editorial board. The complex politics of editorship, with their edgings-in, squeezings-out, and buddings-off, helped, like travel and gardening, to make Gide a practical man (there is no better repose, this side excess, from the ravages of creation), and, more important, to give him the sense of action, of living in this world. It is very likely that the launching of the *N R F ,* by making him feel that even when he was not writing he was being useful, played an important part in setting Gide to writing again.

But the main trend of this crucial decade of reaction from *Fruits of the Earth,* of recoil in order to leap better, was a desire to 'settle down'. Both moral and artistic motives were at work in this deliberate cultivation of anchorages – moral, because he wished to regain, by a respectable married life, the self-respect that Michel had lost, and artistic, because he meant to create greater works than were possible to an unmatured wanderer and immoralist. The influence of his wife was powerful here, growing because of its very silence. The abandoning of La Roque in 1900 was another step in this direction. We may conjecture that Gide's reasons for deserting his mother's home may have been, in part, similar to Michel's in selling La Morinière – but it also prevented the unsettling oscillation of the 1890s between La Roque and Cuverville. Cuverville, until the exile of the Second World War, became his home for the greater part of each year. Here, like Voltaire's Candide at the end of *his* wandering, he cultivated his garden. Even more than the acclimatization of exotic shrubs and flowers, he enjoyed pruning, grafting, training, and transplanting. He was making practical investigation into the benefits of constraint; in his creative life he felt himself to be both gardener and plant. A less successful attempt to take root was the building of his huge and expensive house at Auteuil, which he began in 1904 and occupied in February 1906. His very thrift, he must have felt, would compel him to make use of this earthly mansion and keep him from wandering. 'I expect from this house the energy I shall put into my work, my genius,' he wrote. But the uninhabitable Villa Montmorency became a mere *pied à terre,* a monument to the impossibility of living in Paris, 'a villa without master'.

Gide had written nothing for two years, when in October 1903 he landed in North Africa, for the sixth time, to collect materials for a travel book. What was his purpose in writing *Amyntas?* Certainly it was neither political nor social. 'The gravest economical and ethnological questions were to be raised in the book,' he says; 'I took with me notebooks that I meant to fill with precise documentation and statistics. . . . Can these be the same notebooks that you see here?' In fact, both economics and people are nearly absent from *Amyntas.* Even Athman, now a vain, magnificently dressed young man of twenty-five, rarely enters (next year he married and disappeared from Gide's life). For the most part Gide wanders alone through the Tunisian autumn, and his book is a round of the three symbolic attractions of North Africa, café, oasis, and desert; desert, oasis, and café. He says little of himself – the country speaks for him through its sights, like 'the

little flute with four stops, through which the ennui of the desert
tells its tale. . . . I should like these phrases to be for you what this
flute, and the desert, were to me – a varied monotony.'

A varied monotony – can this be the same Tunisia that gave
him life and liberation in 1893? The Tunisia of *Amyntas* is that of
Michel's second journey. Beauty is still everywhere, but the spirit
of delight has fled. Often Gide tries to find objective reasons, in
newly paved streets or vulgarized cafés, for his disappointment.
It is now autumn, with lifeless heat followed by icy wind and grey
skies – his other journeys had been into spring. Yet he had *chosen*
to go into autumn. He brought the season with him – the autumn
(though only for a time, for Gide's life was to have many autumns
and many springs) is now in his heart. 'Murmurs of gardens, per-
fumes, trees, I recognize them all – the only unrecognizable thing
is myself.' 'One understands better, perhaps, but the amazed enchantment is gone.' Sometimes he recognizes the cause: 'Anguish
is in ourselves only,' he writes to his wife, 'this country, on the
contrary, is utterly calm.' Sometimes ravishment returns: 'I address
my devotions this morning to the Apollo of the Sahara, whom I
see with gilded hair, black limbs, and eyes of porcelain. This morning my joy is perfect.' But mostly he can hope for a no less sad
delight than when, in the café at Biskra, he smokes a little hashish
and finds 'a well-being composed not of the satisfaction of desire,
but of its vanishing, of total renunciation.'

'Obsessed by the desire of this country, and wishing at last to be
cured of it, I wrote this book *pro remedio animae meae,* for the
remedy of my soul.' It is not always easy. Even now he still finds
something new, and cries: 'I had not noticed this the other year –
ah, am I going to wish to return?' 'Abruptly here and there some
crumb of delight reveals an aftertaste so mysterious, that I feel myself without the courage to break away from this country.' But
the victory had been won before he set out. The magic of Tunisia
was spent in him, and its room was needed; the pomegranate had
changed to a useless lotus. *Amyntas* is an acknowledgment and a
cancellation of his debt to desert and oasis, a homeopathic antidote
to wandering. And he called the chief section of his book 'The
Renunciation of Travel'.

After a month his wife joined him. From Algiers he watched the sea that would bring her, and wrote: 'My gaze invents the path and furrow of your ship – why cannot it reach even to Marseilles! May the sea bear you mildly, may the movement of the waves be pleasant to you!' *Amyntas,* almost alone of his books,[1] is dedicated to her. Then he committed himself to her and to Cuverville, where next autumn he wrote: 'The stormwind from the North beats at my window. Oh, how beautiful were the caravans, when in the evening at Touggourt the sun sank to rest in the salt-lake!'

In the post-factum re-classification of his works in 1914 Gide placed *Amyntas* with his poetry. The prose of *Amyntas* has none of the hidden alexandrines that grace *Fruits of the Earth,* but it is adorned with poetic inversions, rare enough to be always unexpected, and an interesting innovation in so uninflected a language as French. But even in French the verbs are highly inflected, and Gide brings off many of his effects by the dexterous placing of the verb. It is significant that during this journey he was re-reading Virgil's Eclogues, in which he found the same verbal pointillism, the pastoral heat and shade, the pervading yet elusive melancholy that inform his book. There, too, he found his title, as he had found the names of Ménalque and Tityrus, and was to take that of Corydon.

> Were I like you a shepherd, for me too
> Would Phyllis garlands wreathe, Amyntas sing—

and Virgil adds, 'What matter, if Amyntas is dark-skinned?' – heartfelt words which Gide had used as epigraph to Book Seven of *Fruits of the Earth.*

[1] The others are *Strait is the Gate,* in some editions, and *Dostoevsky.*

5

THE RE-DEPARTURE OF THE PRODIGAL

The Return of the Prodigal Son, Strait is the Gate, Isabelle

'Knowing how to free oneself is nothing; the difficulty is knowing how to *be* free'. – *The Immoralist.*

In December 1905 began a momentous series of meetings with Paul Claudel, back from his Chinese consulship for a year's leave among the heathen French. He had landed the previous May, and soon joined Francis Jammes, then suffering in his Pyrenean home from the agonizing end of a three-years-old love-affair. The young girl's parents had opposed their marriage; she had threatened to take the veil, and then, in July, she married, as poor Jammes wrote to Gide, 'a gentleman who resides at Suez.' Claudel seized the opportunity to convert Jammes. They took communion side by side, and went on pilgrimage to Lourdes. Jammes had always been a good Catholic, and henceforth he became, like Claudel, a militant. In December Claudel went after still bigger game; and at no time in his life more than now, at the apogee of his retreat from *Fruits of the Earth*, was Gide ready to duel with a hunter of souls. Even before their meeting he had written to Jammes, knowing he would pass the information to Claudel: 'I pondered for a long time whether I should try to meet him when he was still in Paris; but it seemed I could only have received him worthily in a certain secret room, to whose door I have long lost the key, though you know I am trying to reopen it.' But when they met, Gide was on the defensive. In 1900 Claudel 'looked like a nail –

now he looks like a hammer,' – or, Gide adds, 'like a coagulated cyclone.' However, Gide asked him to lunch, where Claudel spoke of God, Catholicism, his faith, and his happiness therein. Gide was moved, and said, 'I understand you.' 'Then why don't you become converted?' retorted Claudel, and left Gide the address of his confessor. The assault was continued in conversation and letter, and in the following March the combatants had 'an explanation'. 'It was not communion with the eucharist, but communion with Claudel that attracted me,' Gide wrote to Jammes; 'if he has his God, I have mine, and it was an impious weakness that led me so to separate myself from Him.' Claudel returned to China, but Jammes tactlessly tried to succeed where his master had failed. A year of unrest followed for Gide, who must have felt like a cannibal captured by missionaries. He was steering his cousin Paul Gide through a difficult love-affair, to say nothing of one of his own with a certain M., and the early stages of *Strait is the Gate* were giving trouble. He suffered from insomnia and mental fatigue, consulted Dr Andreæ at Geneva in May, and rested in Brittany in August. In February 1907, on a sudden inspiration, he wrote *Le Retour de l'Enfant prodigue (The Return of the Prodigal Son)*, one of the few among his major works that came without years of conscious meditation.

Gide's parable begins where the Gospel's ends. What happened in the prodigal's home after the fatted calf was eaten, and was the angry brother satisfied, when the Father told him, 'this thy brother was dead, and is alive again'? Gide's prodigal had fled from home not to seek lawless joys, but 'to buy fervour at the price of all I possessed.' His truant years were spent not in riotous living, but in the desert, where he sought and found destitution. He is no immoralist, but the wanderer of *Fruits* and *Amyntas* come exhausted home.

On the day after the feast the Father reprimands him. 'Why did you leave me?' The prodigal replies that in the desert he had felt nearer to his Father than in his Father's House – for 'You made the earth, but others built the House in your name.' And the Father admits that he has spoken only as the elder brother bade him; 'for here it is he who makes the Law.' Next day it is the brother's turn.

'The Father no longer explains himself clearly,' he says, 'and he who wishes to understand the Father must listen to me.' Freedom and sacrifice lead to chaos, he alleges; we must hold fast to what we have. The model of human existence is already perfected, and we must not depart from it. 'Enter into the repose of the House,' he concludes kindly, and the prodigal consents: 'I will gladly, because I am weary.'

The day after, he talks with his mother. 'I went away to discover who I was,' he stammers. 'You are the son of your parents and brother of your brothers,' she tells him. She is anxious about her youngest son,[1] who resembles the prodigal, and fears he, too, may leave her. On the fourth night the prodigal obeys his mother and goes to warn his little brother of the dangers of liberty. On the table by his bed the child has a pomegranate, fruit of the earth *par excellence*! He is leaving that very night, and the prodigal, in bitter admiration, gives his blessing: 'You take all my hopes with you. Be strong, forget us, forget me. May you be able not to return.'

Gide's fable is highly ambiguous, for it crystallizes an ambiguous state of mind. In his mother's lifetime he had been all restraint, since 1893 he had been all freedom; henceforth restraint and freedom, in growing harmony, were to co-exist in him. It would be mistaken to see only satire in the 'poem' of the prodigal. Its tone is reverent, even devotional, as well as ironic. Even in the opportunism of the elder brother's words there is much that is dignified and fine, much that is not only true, but felt as true by Gide. The parable reflects not only Gide's victory over Claudel, but his desire to submit, his vision, renounced but remembered, of the healing repose and authorized joys of Claudel's God's House.

The House is not Heaven, as in the Gospel, but the Universal Catholic Church. The elder brother is the militant priest, and the Father is not God himself, but God interpreted by the priest. It detracts from the universality of Gide's parable that God is not allowed to speak for Himself. And yet for one moment Gide's own Protestant God shows through, to say, 'I know what drove you

---

[1] In Luke xiv there are only two brothers.

on your way, and I awaited you at the end – you had only to call Me.' 'My Father,' cries the prodigal, 'then I might have found You without returning?'

On a more personal level the House is Cuverville, and the desert that surrounds it is Tunisia. The elder brother is Claudel, and the younger brother is the type of the real-life Nathanaels who, now that Gide was returning to discipline, were beginning to listen to his doctrine of freedom. But the prodigal is not Gide himself. Where the prodigal had surrendered, Gide had vanquished Claudel; and it was to a different house that he returned, not the House of Claudel's God, but his own Cuverville. Yet his homecoming was a real one. Though he was to set out again, it was never with the utter cap-in-air freedom of the decade of *Fruits of the Earth*. He was committed now to Cuverville, to work and self-imposed restraint, and his future wanderings were perhaps the richer thereby. He was no longer 'a kite that thinks it could climb higher without its string.' Home he has come – but he still maintains that his journey was really necessary, and for others as well as himself. Conversion was to his middle years what immoralism had been to his youth: a grave temptation which he overcame by abandoning to a book the fragment of himself that surrendered.

The unforeseen compulsion from Claudel to meditate on God, and what Man has made of Him (a subject untreated in Gide's work since the Millionaire of *Prometheus*), may have released some inhibition in the writing of *La Porte étroite (Strait is the Gate)*, which had been hanging fire since its commencement in June 1905. From June 1907, when Gide rewrote its opening chapters for the fourth time, his novel went more smoothly. He finished it on 15 October 1908, and the next day shaved, for ever, his moustache! 'My poor André, you must see your mistake,' said his wife – but this burlesque incident had its purpose. Gide had made in his novel a final farewell to the past. He and his face now had nothing to hide behind, and the ironic curves of his art and lips could be bared for all to see.

Strait is the Gate had been evolving in Gide's mind since long before 1905. It had been called variously *Treatise of the Good Death*, or *The Death of Mlle Claire*, was to tell of 'a soul that thinks it has

not adored properly,' and was first suggested by the lonely extinction of Miss Anna Shackleton. She had died in May 1884, ten
days after the fourteen-year-old Gide and his mother took her to a
nursing-home. 'I imagined,' he writes in his autobiography, 'the
desperate cry of this loving soul, abandoned of all save God; and
it is the echo of this cry that sounds in the last pages of *Strait is the
Gate.*' He wrote part of his novel before the mirror of Miss
Shackleton's dressing-table, inherited from his mother. But it was
a very different spinster who in *Strait is the Gate* was to die in the
bare cell of a nursing-home, and even God was to desert her.

At the opening of *Strait is the Gate* we are on the familiar ground
of Gide's youth. Jerome, a serious young Protestant, is in love with
Alissa Bucolin, his cousin at Le Havre. One evening he steals up to
her room, finds her kneeling in tears, and dedicates his life to her
happiness. Alissa has discovered the infidelity of her mother, who
shortly after absconds with a lover. Next Sunday Pastor Vautier,
the family friend, 'no doubt intentionally,' preaches a sermon on
the text from St Luke: 'Enter ye in at the strait gate, for wide is
the gate that leadeth unto destruction, and many there be that go
in thereat: But strait is the gate that leadeth unto life, and few
there be that find it.' And the lives of the cousins are ruled by their
differing interpretations of this text.

Jerome imagines the strait gate as very like the door of his
cousin's room, and the narrow way as just wide enough for two;
but to Alissa it is only wide enough for one. At first she says they
are too young to be engaged, then she discovers that her sister
Juliette is also in love with Jerome, and effaces herself. Juliette
finds happiness in a second-best marriage, but still Alissa will not
accept Jerome. She has turned, it seems, from him to God, and
has offered their love as a sacrifice for their salvation.

There is a last meeting at the little gate in the garden wall of the
Bucolins' country house, Fongueusemare (a gate which exists to
this day at Gide's Cuverville) – it is the earthly form of the narrow
gate of heaven, through which they cannot enter side by side.
'To have forced the gate,' says Jerome, 'to have entered by any
means whatever into the house – no, even today, when I look
back to the past and live it over again – no, it was not possible to

me, and whoever does not understand me here, has understood nothing of me up to now.' Alissa goes to a Paris nursing-home to die alone, and leaves Jerome her journal, in which lies the secret of her sacrifice, for which, like him, we have now to search. *Strait is the Gate* is a mystery novel, and one that remains mysterious however often it is read. But the customary view, that it is a tragedy of young love ruined by religious austerity, is nearly as shortsighted as that of Francis Jammes, who saw Jerome as the villain of the piece, whose efforts to seduce Alissa from divine union were happily thwarted.

Jerome, as is artistically necessary, is something of a nonentity. With less resignation he would have forced Alissa to surrender, or have found some other interest in life, and in either case the novel would have had a different unhappy ending. As it is, Alissa is able so to play on his chivalry, and a love of sacrifice inferior only to her own, as to keep him always at a safe distance; and yet she never discourages him so completely as to drive him away before the sacrifice is ready, and she can offer up to God both her love and his. And Jerome believes to the end that each fending-off is a trial, which will be rewarded by her surrender. 'Against the snare of virtue I remained defenceless,' he says – 'heroism attracted me, because I could not separate it from love.' He follows her upward, thinking to corner her at the mountain-top – but Alissa foils him even there, by hurling herself from the summit, possibly to soar to heaven, probably not.

Alissa's journal shows that her love for Jerome was even greater than Jerome's for her, and at her moments of severest rigour she was nearest giving in. She loved Jerome more than God, and herself more than Jerome, and her virtual suicide is a last attempt to hide this from herself. But it is also an unconscious revenge on her lover. Wiser than Jerome, she knows that he loves not her, but the personality, so like his own, that he has imposed upon her. 'Our letters were a huge mirage,' she tells him, 'and we were writing not to each other but to ourselves.' In wounded pride she takes revenge by raising herself still higher, to a peak of virtue far above the ideal he has invented for her. But, in renouncing her lover, she has destroyed her will to live, and has lost moreover the recompense she hoped to find in after-life. On her deathbed she realizes too late that she is unready to die, and that God, who will not be mocked, had not accepted her sacrifice. The strait gate, she truly foresaw, will not admit two together: but it will not admit even one who clings still to the burdens of earth. It is too narrow for the rich man with his wealth, and too narrow for a soul that has refused to lay down its pride.

Poor Alissa has reached, by going the other way round the world, a damnation very similar to the Immoralist's – indeed, *Strait is the Gate* might be called *The Moralist*. Hers is a greater perversity than Michel's, who, after all, was only doing as he liked. Alissa is doing what she does not like, and at each act of monstrous virtue her anguish increases, till at last it kills her. And yet, her vision of heavenly joy is so surpassingly beautiful as almost to justify its means. In the limited sense in which the Immoralist was right in sinning for earthly joy, Alissa was justified in sinning to achieve her Pisgah view, however false, of heaven. And each pays the exact price – spiritual death for Michel, bodily death and worse for Alissa. 'Whom can I persuade that this book is the twin of *The Immoralist*,' Gide wrote in his *Journal*, 'that the two subjects grew up together in my mind, the excess of the one finding a secret permission in the excess of the other, so that the two together form an equipoise?'[1] Possibly his wife may have seen this intention, without being persuaded of its validity. 'I wrote all my books before *The Coiners*,' he recorded long afterwards,[2] 'under the influence of Madeleine, or in the vain hope of convincing her.' *Strait is the Gate* taps the unassuaged memory of Gide's unsuccessful wooing of his cousin between 1888 and 1891 – it is *André Walter* with a new assessment of the guilty party. Gide is telling his wife that, if the message of *The Immoralist* is 'There, but for the grace of God, go I,' then the message of *Strait is the Gate* is, equally, 'There, but for the grace of God, go you'; or, 'if I admit that my position has its potential dangers, then you should realize that so, too, has yours.'

The public saw none of the complexities that lay beneath the

[1] *Journal*, 7 February 1912.
[2] *Journal*, 9 June 1928.

classically simple surface of this most immediately charming of Gide's novels. It is the most exquisite example in French literature of that favourite idyll, love in the château. The formidable Alissa has the enchanting innocence of a Turgenev heroine, and Gide's feeling for nature in Normandy never surpassed the beauty of Fongueusemare and its seasons, of which Jammes quaintly remarked: 'I cannot describe it all here, for I should have to enumerate every leaf, and the book contains three hundred.' To the consternation of all, the book began to sell; and Gide's publishers, the *Mercure de France*, were not least taken aback. Having printed the unusually large edition, for Gide, of a thousand copies, they had distributed the type; but in two months a new edition was needed. Perhaps the desire to avoid similar contretemps entered into the founding of the *N R F*'s own publishing house, under Gallimard, in 1911. The new firm became Gide's exclusive publishers, beginning in the same year with *Isabelle*; and Gide became, if not a popular author, an unpopular author who sold well.

We are approaching the years in which Gide became a great novelist, and we shall be delayed, as Gide was himself, by an intervening work which at first seems irrelevant, but is in fact the medium of a crucial transition. He was not sure, when he began *Isabelle* in April 1910,[1] that it was the work he ought then to be writing. He disliked the subtle shading of its style, and longed for the gaiety and flat tones of the prose he foresaw for *The Vatican Swindle*. But *Isabelle* was a preliminary, small-scale exercise in writing about other people, and directing to an impersonal plot the storytelling genius he had acquired through autobiographical fiction. The narrative brilliance of Mérimée, whom he had re-read in the previous year, stood by him here; but he softened its hardness with the wet, green Normandy landscape, that would not have attracted Mérimée, who knew no middle term between Mediterranean and Baltic. From Mérimée, too,[2] came the device of the narrator who visits a country house, scents a mystery, and sets out to solve it. But Gide took his plot from local history. The

---

[1] Finished 12 November 1910. See *Journal* for 14 November.
[2] Notably in *La Vénus d'Ille* and his little-known masterpiece, *Lokis*.

subtle blending of imaginative and actual truth, even now that he
had abandoned autobiography, was to remain a primary theme
of his fiction.

In September 1898 Francis Jammes had visited La Roque. 'I was
given a room of the most spectral kind, in a ruined tower, where
one morning I found a young owl in my slipper,' he recorded[1] –
though once his solitude was enlivened by a more welcome
visitor, a beautiful female apparition who glided down the moon-
beams to his bed. One day Gide took him to a ruined country
house near by, and told him its story. That night Jammes composed
his superb but romanticized Fourth Elegy:

> Since you have asked me for an elegy
> On this deserted manor where the wind . . .

And twelve years later, in *Isabelle*, Gide wrote the hideously
tragic truth.[2] Gérard, a young scholar, arrives at Quartfourche
(the name means Crossroads – 'what happens if one takes the
wrong turning?' he wonders), where he finds four fossilized old
people, with the family priest and a crippled, feeble-minded boy.
Poor Casimir is without visible parents, and we imagine goodness
knows what dark history of seduction of the heiress by the abbé,
or the gardener, or incest . . . but the scent is false, and the parentage of Casimir is not the heart of the mystery. Gérard sees a
portrait of the boy's mother, and falls in love with her angelic
innocence. In a deserted summer-house in the park he finds the
letter she had written to her lover on the eve of their elopement,
and the abbé reveals that the young Vicomte was shot on the fatal
night, fifteen years before, by Gratien the gardener. What must
Isabelle's anguish have been as she waited for the lover who never
came! Casimir's deformity was caused by her efforts to conceal
her pregnancy, before her parents cast her off. On the last night of
Gérard's visit Isabelle, beautiful still but fallen, arrives to demand

---

[1] 'All that is charming,' Gide commented acidly, 'but a little truth would have
been even more interesting.'

[2] Isabelle, the old relatives, the crippled child, the sale of timber, Isabelle's final
degradation, and many minor details, are all taken from real life. Quartfourche was
the château of Formentin, near La Roque. Gide knew 'Casimir', but never met
'Isabelle', who died in 1894.

money from the old people. Gérard spies on her, but is unable to contrive an interview.

Next spring Gérard returns, to find the old people dead, and Isabelle in possession. The house is to be sold for debt, but Isabelle, by sleeping with the creditors' agent, has succeeded in selling the trees in the park for five francs each.[1] Her fallen state only attracts Gérard the more. He declares his love, and confronts her with the long-lost letter; and breaking down at the sight of this visitant from the past, Isabelle tells him the lost secret. On the night of her elopement she was seized with terror of the liberty she had desired so long. Without courage to tell the Vicomte of her decision, she asked Gratien to intercept him; and Gratien was overzealous, with the result we know. Isabelle's grief is all for herself, none for her murdered lover; and now recovering her self-possession, she hints to the horrified Gérard that she is ready to receive his advances. The love of Isabelle de Saint-Auréol is within his grasp – but the reality is too unlike the dream. He leaves hastily, and Isabelle makes do with a coachman. 'She always had to have somebody,' says Gratien.

De te fabula. Gide had not yet discovered Browning, but *Isabelle* is the story of *The Statue and the Bust*, with Browning's self-same moral, that when the heart's only vital instinct is to sin, abstinence may be the greater crime. Through once refusing to give way to her temptation, Isabelle lost her only chance of virtue, and all in vain; for how often afterwards did she take her mother's jewels and follow lover after lover! But the hidden theme of Gide's tale is more sombre still. He has shown us nothing less than the breakdown of romantic love. Gérard's love of Isabelle is even more instructive than the murdered Vicomte's. He has fallen in love with a face, and, for seeking to find the truth behind it, has found a harlot. Better the love of the senses or no love at all, than the lying vision in another of something higher than oneself! Gide rarely returned to the theme – it was enough, for him, to tuck it away in a minor novel – yet, by its very absence, it is implicit in all his work. The hollowness of nineteenth-century love, whether we accept it or not, is one of the paramount motifs of

---

[1] 'And they're worth a hundred and twenty apiece,' says old Gratien, weeping.

the twentieth century. So far no new illusion has been invented to take its place; and Gide would probably say that we can, and should, do without it altogether. It is no coincidence that Isabelle's face in the miniature is very like Alissa's, very like Marceline's.

6

CRIME WITHOUT PUNISHMENT

The Vatican Swindle

'This abominable effort to carry one's sins with one to paradise.' – *Journal* 1913.

No great event marked the liberation of Gide's now mature genius for a major novel. The past decade of influence and restraint, his renunciation of travel and other liquidations of the past, the writing of *The Immoralist* and *Strait is the Gate*, had been preparations; and he wrote *The Vatican Swindle* when these preparations were completed. He began it in October 1911, and finished on 23 June 1913.

So much of the action takes place in railway trains, that it seems fitting to begin and end our study of the novel with relevant anecdotes of Gide in a railway carriage. In October 1911, on Friday the 13th – 'it had to be that,' he records in his *Journal* – he 'travelled beside a little whore in spectacles, who kept the whole compartment awake till half-past one in the morning, reading *A Woman's Kiss*. Too exasperated to sleep, especially as I didn't dare say anything cutting to her on account of the fat protector who dozed opposite.' From this irritation over an affair of electric light in a railway carriage Gide drew an important incident of his novel.

Anthime Armand-Dubois, an atheist, Freemason, and vivisector of rats, has come to Rome to cure his sciatica. 'You would do better to cure your soul,' says his brother-in-law Julius. Anthime's 'free' thought is as superficial and trammelled as Julius's faith.

The Madonna appears to him in a dream and heals both his un-
belief and his hip joint. He walks without crutches, and is hailed
by the Catholic world as a distinguished convert.

Anthime's wife's sister's husband, Count Julius de Baraglioul, a
novelist, Catholic and would-be Academician, is ordered by his
dying father, a retired ambassador, to investigate the character of a
certain Lafcadio Wluiki. Lafcadio's temporary mistress, Carola,
lets Julius into her lover's room, where he dutifully reads the
young man's journal, and is surprised in the act. Though only
nineteen, Lafcadio is already a Nietzschean superman. He is
blond, handsome, steel-strong in body and will, and whenever
he inadvertently betrays his true feelings, he punishes himself by
plunging a penknife into his thigh. His mother was a high-class
courtesan, and he has been brought up by her successive lovers.
Lafcadio and Julius realize simultaneously that they are half-
brothers. Lafcadio dismisses Carola and meets Julius's daughter
Geneviève, who falls in love with him. The old ambassador dies,
leaving his bastard a fortune.

Lafcadio's former school-friend, Protos, disguised as a priest,
visits Julius's sister, Comtesse Valentine de Saint-Prix. The Pope,
he explains, has been imprisoned by Freemasons, and an impostor
reigns in his place. He collects a donation of 60,000 francs towards
the crusade to free the Holy Father, and swears the countess to
absolute secrecy. She hastens to inform her sister-in-law, Arnica
Fleurissoire, younger sister of the wives of Julius and Anthime,
who tells her husband Amédée. This good-hearted simpleton is
the most practical Christian of the family; for he sets off for Rome
to rescue the Pope.

The first night Amédée battles with bugs, the second with
fleas, the third with mosquitoes. One of the gang meets his train
at Rome, and takes him to a dubious hotel, that turns out to be a
brothel where Protos lives with Carola. His fourth night is
equally sleepless, for Carola seduces him (though a married man
he was still a virgin); and he is overcome by remorse, feeling he
is no longer worthy to accomplish his mission. Carola gives him
her cuff-links, a keepsake from Lafcadio, and warns Protos not to
harm him. Amédée has a letter of introduction to a genuine cardinal

in Naples, but Protos takes him to a fellow-impostor, and sends him back to Rome to cash a cheque. There he finds Julius, who has just lost his faith, having interviewed the Pope unsuccessfully on behalf of Anthime, who glories in the Christian poverty to which Freemasons and Church alike have left him. Julius is unconvinced by Amédée's explanation, that the real Pope is not to blame. Some premonition makes Amédée ask Julius to accompany him to Naples; Julius refuses, but helps his doomed brother-in-law to cash his cheque, and lends him his return ticket.

Amédée joins the carriage in which Lafcadio, now a rich man, is on his way to embark for Borneo. The atrocious stripling is on the look-out for the unforeseen, for the chance of an irrational act. Irritated by Fleurissoire's mediocre appearance and his juggling with the electric light, he opens the carriage door and pushes him out, carrying with him, alas, Lafcadio's pride and joy, his new beaver hat, complete with the address of his hatter. Lafcadio is amazed to find Julius's name on Fleurissoire's ticket, still more amazed to read next day that the corpse has been found wearing Carola's cuff-links, and, oddest of all, that someone has cut the hatter's name from the hat. 'The old man was a crossroads,' mutters Lafcadio. He returns to Rome, and finds Julius exalted with an idea for his new novel. He has resolved to explore the psychological profundities of an irrational act, and welcomes a heaven-sent example thereof in the murder of his brother-in-law ('this providential adventure,' he calls it, and refers to the murderer as 'my hero') – were it not that the motive was evidently robbery. This is too much for Lafcadio, who points out in the stop-press of his newspaper that Fleurissoire's 6000 francs were found intact in the railway carriage. Julius is incapable of recognizing an irrational act when he sees one. If the motive was not robbery, then Amédée's story was true, and the deceased is a martyr for the Pope. His faith returns accordingly; but feeling that now he knows the appalling secret he is in the same danger, he persuades Lafcadio to bring back the body from Naples in his stead.

On the train a passenger engages Lafcadio in conversation, and speaks of the restraint of social convention, of crime as a release

therefrom, and the particular freedom of the bastard! Such is the
nightmare of this sinister dialogue, that Lafcadio is positively relieved when his tormentor turns out to be Protos in disguise. He
has seen the murder and suppressed the incriminating hat-label,
and he tries to intimidate Lafcadio into joining the gang and black-
mailing Julius. 'Excuse me if I prefer the police to you,' replies
Lafcadio.

At the funeral the newly devout Julius tells Anthime the secret
of the false pope; and Anthime, enraged to think he has suffered in
vain, instantly returns to Freemasonry, and limps again. Protos is
denounced by Carola, who believes he is the murderer of her
beloved Fleurissoire, and when the police arrive he strangles her.
Lafcadio reveals his crime to Julius, who, with mild severity, advises him to reform and go to confession. Geneviève overhears,
and comes to Lafcadio's room to beg him to escape. He announces
that he will give himself up to the police, and overcome by the
prospect of losing him, she throws herself into his arms. The novel
ends at dawn, when Lafcadio rises to contemplate, not his sleeping
beloved, but the wakening city. 'What, is he going to renounce his
life?' asks Gide. 'For the esteem of Geneviève, which he values a
little less now she loves him a little more, does he still think of
giving himself up?'

To understand what *The Vatican Swindle* is about, we must discover what Gide was thinking and doing when the novel was
coming into being. There are two main plots in *The Vatican
Swindle*: the story of Lafcadio and the story of the conspiracy;
and they are linked by the relationship of the family on which
they both react. The first mention of the novel in Gide's *Journal*
is a note for 20 January 1902 on 'the novel I am dreaming
about, concerning the relations between a dozen characters.'
Shortly before, on 5 January, he remarked: 'Great crimes have
sometimes been committed so easily only because they happened
as in a dream. Afterwards the criminal would have liked to wake
up, or not to have been taken so seriously.' This thought later
occurred to Lafcadio! – and both passages are embedded in a
nexus of possible living models for Lafcadio. But whence came
the idea of the swindle?

The conspiracy owes much to the nihilist gang of Dostoevsky's *The Possessed*, just as Protos[1] recalls the abominable Pyotr Verkhovensky. But the Vatican swindlers are unburdened with the metaphysical and apocalyptic aims of the Possessed; their object is not to destroy, but to make a fool of society. Protos is an artist in crime – he swindles not for trafficking alone, and adorns his snares with all manner of beautiful but useless arabesques of intrigue and irony. Murder is not among his perversions; Verkhovensky killed Shatov, but it is Lafcadio who kills Fleurissoire.

However, there was indeed a Vatican Swindle, which occurred in 1893, the very year in which Gide's novel is set. A crooked lawyer, an unfrocked nun and a scandalous priest conspired at Lyons to spread the rumour that Leo XIII had been imprisoned by Freemason cardinals who had substituted a false Pope in his place, and collected money from the faithful for his release. There is no need, therefore, to doubt the recollection of Paul Laurens, who remembered Gide speaking of his future novel at Biskra in 1893, nearly twenty years before it was written; though Gide, in his *Journal* for 25 September 1913, remarks: 'That is further back than I remembered.' For the conversion of Anthime Armand-Dubois Gide used the equally true incident of a Freemason cousin of Émile Zola, who abjured his atheism at a public ceremony in the church of Il Gesù at Rome, just as did poor Anthime. In so far as *The Vatican Swindle* is a study of man's ever-thwarted relations with God, its subject is not unconnected with the seriocomic contest between Gide's Prometheus and the millionaire-Zeus, and other similar themes in Gide's ideas and works of the 1890s. Gide collected newspaper-cuttings about the swindle in 1893, but postponed his novel for two decades, during which a multitude of further themes congregated about this fantastic but factual nucleus.

The real existence of the 1893 conspiracy is not the only element of topicality in Gide's fiction. Leo XIII, from his strained relations

---

[1] His bantering manner, dandyism, exquisite prose, hand-made slang, practical jokes, and domination of his school-fellow, recall Pierre Louÿs, who at the time when the novel appeared was already slowly dying of tertiary syphilis. Pierre=Pyotr=Protos.

with the crown of Italy, was known as 'the prisoner of the Vatican.' He was a vigorous opponent of the Freemasons, and on 10 January 1890 issued the encyclical *Sapientiae Christianae* approving the French Republic, of which Protos hypocritically remarks, 'Imagine, madam, how the captive Pontiff must have suffered, to hear this impostor proclaim him a republican!' Possibly, however, a casual remark of Francis Jammes, in a letter of March 1898 to Gide then at Rome, may have started the train of thought that led to his renewed interest in the Swindle. 'Does the Pope know you are in Rome?' Jammes inquired, with a levity that would have horrified him a few years later – 'and is it true that the Great White Chief feeds on nothing but the scent of roses?'

Another parallel is perhaps only an astonishing coincidence. Gide prefixed to the section of the novel that introduces the conspiracy a quotation from Claudel's play, *L'Annonce faite à Marie*: 'Of what king speak you, and of what pope? For there are two, and no one knows which is the real one.'[1] Claudel's play was published in 1914, and written, it is said, in 1912, too late to suggest any fundamental addition to Gide's novel; and the passage does not occur in the earlier versions of his play, those of 1892 and 1900. It is just possible that Claudel's '1912' version was in fact begun earlier, and seen by Gide during Claudel's home leave in 1905.[2] Certainly Claudel was not himself quoting Gide; he insisted on the withdrawal of the compromising epigraph, attempted again to convert Gide, and broke with him finally.

Claudel's assault on Gide's soul in 1905 was of paramount importance in the novel, and supplied by reaction, if not its subject, much of the energy that went to its creation. Before 1905 Catholicism was a matter of indifference to Gide: the pursuit of God had appeared in all his writings, the flight from Catholicism in none. After 1905 he saw the Church as an enemy to both pans of the 'Gidian balance': as a menace to his spiritual freedom and a temptation to his love of restraint. How seductive was the temptation is

---

[1] A reference to the Great Schism in the fourteenth century, when there were two claimants to the Papacy.

[2] The title *Les Caves*, which presupposes the conspiracy, first appears in the *Journal* of 3 September 1905, after Claudel's capture of Jammes, but before his raid on Gide.

visible in the beauty and sincerity of Anthime's conversion,[1] so excessive in view of the sudden ease of his apostasy, that the discrepancy may be felt as one of the few flaws in the novel. Against the menace he defended himself by satirical attack. Is not Protos's vast confidence-trick an allegory of the Church? Would not the believer's faith remain identical, Gide implies, if the Pope had always been a usurper? And if the faithful are so easily taken in about the Pope, may they not be equally deceived about the true nature of God?

It would seem that there is no need to seek a source in real life for Lafcadio. He is, very evidently, Dostoevsky's Raskolnikov, crossed with two heroes of Stendhal, Julien Sorel for pride and Fabrice del Dongo for gaiety and resource. Yet we are faced with the presence in Gide's life, during the incubation of his novel, of a positive embarrassment of possible Lafcadios. First there are *louche* young characters whom Gide met during his period of prowling on the boulevards: Alexandre S., a crook and gigolo, pale, delicately beautiful, and Spanish-looking – Gide met him in 1898, and again in 1902, when he was nineteen, Lafcadio's age; or Émile X., a tailor's son, with whom Gide frequented a public swimming bath – Gide's word-portrait of him recalls the nude photograph that Julius finds on Lafcadio's mantelpiece. And the *Journal* gives glimpses of other more important and still more shadowy figures later in the decade: M. in 1905, Armand in 1909, and yet others whose only name is a letter of the alphabet. Somewhere among these is the hidden source of the emotion that created Lafcadio *con amore*.[2] Outside Gide's more private life, other personages appear, make some gesture or speech that belongs to Lafcadio, and vanish. In June 1904 the sinister young hero[3] of Gide's 'Conversation with a German' comes straight from prison to visit him and say: 'Action is what I desire – the most intense

---

[1] The Virgin also appeared, much to Gide's amusement, to Émile Baumann, a Catholic novelist. See *Journal* for 7 June 1912.

[2] Cocteau, no doubt with good reason, identified their mutual young friend, the mysterious and shady Arthur Cravan, as the model for Lafcadio and for Julius's visit to Lafcadio's room.

[3] An entry in the *Journal* for 18 January 1932 shows that he was Félix-Paul Grève, Gide's German translator.

action . . . even murder.' And Gide, embarrassed but enthralled, replies: 'No, action interests me less by the sensation it gives me, than by its consequences. I hate to limit what I might do, by what I actually do. I would rather cause an action than perform one.' In May 1905 the violent futurist Marinetti calls, and is 'so polite that I had to leave for the country at once – if I'd seen him again, it would have been all up with me, I might have decided he had genius'. And in the train with Fleurissoire, Lafcadio, longing for 'a nice catastrophe, soaked in horror, when they'll push the printed word to hell overboard', echoes the anti-literary platform of Marinetti's Futurist Manifesto of 1909. As for Lafcadio's antecedents, they strongly resemble those of Guillaume Apollinaire, whom Gide discovered in January 1908. Apollinaire's original surname was Kostrowicki (cf. the Rumanian 'Wluiki') after his mother, a courtesan of noble Polish birth. His unknown father was variously supposed to be a brother of the bishop of Monaco, the bishop himself, or a grandson of the great Napoleon. And finally, but not exhaustively, Lafcadio has elements of Lautréamont, terrible author of the *Chants de Maldoror*, and of Rimbaud, both of whom Gide was reading in November 1905. Rimbaud on occasion used words very like Lafcadio's 'Let us leave Europe, and print our naked heel on the ground!' Lafcadio sets out for Borneo, and Rimbaud went to Java.

Except for Protos and Carola, all the characters of *The Vatican Swindle* are members by blood or marriage of one family. In the days when the concept 'family' meant to Gide the repressive and warping power of parents over their children, he had made Ménalque cry, 'Families, I hate you.' When he became, by seniority and wealth, head of his own family of in-laws, nephews, and nieces, he felt differently. He liked to have what he called 'my people' gathered round him at Cuverville, and became a tutor and second father to his nephews, Jacques and Dominique Drouin, and his nieces Nicole and Françoise Gilbert. The sense of family is one of the chief cohesive forces of his novel, and an important constituent of the emotions from which he created it. If we knew more about the Drouins and Gilberts in the 1900s, we should perhaps understand more of what the Baragliouls, Fleurissoires, and Armand-Dubois meant to Gide. But it may be significant that the Gilberts, like the Fleurissoires, lived at Pau; that Nicole and Françoise Gilbert had the same comparative ages as Julius's daughters, Geneviève and Véronique; and that the pious Comtesse de Saint-Prix has the same Christian name as Valentine Gilbert. And the widowed Valentine became in 1911, with Francis Jammes's assistance, the first Catholic in the family for over fifty years.

Not the least important among the foundations of family – and they dwell, where foundations belong, underground – are incest, fratricide, and illegitimacy. It must not escape notice that Julius, who more than once is on the verge of more than brotherly feeling for Lafcadio, is his half-brother; Fleurissoire, whom he murders, is his brother-in-law; and Geneviève, with whom he sleeps, is his niece. Most important of all, Lafcadio is illegitimate: 'You will never be more than a bastard,' says his dying father.

The bastard is, for Gide, a special and ideal case of the free individual. It is the function of parents to give us morality, to replace in us the unborn personality with the generic social type. Our motives henceforth are conventional and imposed from outside, we are incapable of an act of individual significance. But the bastard, by Gide's ironic but instructive theory, having no parents, inheriting no ready-made motivation, will retain his individuality. He will therefore enjoy what, in Gide's paradox, is the highest and rarest form of freedom: he will be capable of a motiveless act!

Did Gide himself believe in the 'gratuitous act'? Presumably not, for he repeatedly denies its existence, and he discusses it through the mouths of burlesque characters, the philosopher Alexandre in *Marshlands*, the waiter in *Prometheus Misbound*, and the ineffable Julius. He believed in it, if at all, not as a fact, but as a fabulous absolute, a moral and aesthetic concept not valid in itself, but showing the way to new discoveries. The gratuitous act is like a pointer on a scientific instrument, indicating some impossibly high figure – it is important not because it is truthful in itself, but because it demands an explanation. Lafcadio shows that Newtonian ethics have broken down.

The gratuitous act is a symbol: philosophically, of freedom; morally, of instantaneous expression of the whole personality; and psychologically, of the break-through of the Id. These three aspects correspond to the adumbrations of gratuity in Bergson, Nietzsche, and Dostoevsky respectively; and all three are present in Lafcadio's defenestration of Fleurissoire. But the moment we investigate the gratuitous act not as a fruitful image but as a real entity, it disintegrates into fallacies. If a really motiveless act were possible, as might be with some lesion of the brain, it would be meaningless – to have any significance it must have a significant cause – and so cease to be gratuitous! And in practical aesthetics, if the novelist is to convince the reader that a gratuitous act has been committed, then he must make it credible by giving it a motive – and once again its gratuity disappears. A gratuitous act is pure only so long as it remains mysterious.

'A gratuitous act,' says the waiter in *Prometheus*, 'is an act unmotivated by passion or interest, born from itself, a means to no end.' And the Millionaire, who is God Almighty, says: 'I alone, who alone possess an infinite fortune, can act with absolute disinterest – mere Man cannot.' But even the Millionaire-God, whose gratuitous act is the famous slap and banknote, is not quite disinterested: he acts, as he confesses, from love of gambling, to see what mankind will make of it. And the act of Lafcadio, a mere mortal, has its hidden causes. He does not know them, attributing his deed, like Zeus the Millionaire, to curiosity and love of risk, and Gide does not state them; but they are clear enough. Lafcadio's illegitimacy has made him an enemy of society. He has simultaneously found and lost his father; his inheritance of 40,000 francs a year of useless money is only a final mockery. His unconscious need for recognition and parental love – it is irrelevant that he is too far gone to know what to do with them if he had them – has turned to equally unconscious need for revenge. In the mediocre bourgeois image of Fleurissoire he pushes overboard the society that has rejected him. The two great 'free acts' in Dostoevsky, to which Lafcadio's is evidently akin, are in fact no less motivated than his. Raskolnikov murders the old pawnbroker as a proof of his moral superiority (she is also, like Fleurissoire, a symbol of society); and Kirillov in *The Possessed* kills himself because, he says, a motiveless suicide is the supreme act of will that can make man become God: and there, precisely, is his motive. When Gide came later to discuss the suicide of Kirillov in his *Dostoevsky*, he called it 'gratuitous, but not without motive'; and re-defined 'gratuitous' as 'without motivation from outside.' By thus restoring logicality to the gratuitous act he detracted from its mystical significance; he made it a riddle with an answer, a specimen of mainly psychological interest.

That *The Vatican Swindle* is, in the fullest Gidian sense, an ironical work, need hardly be stated; and so Gide himself felt, when he wrote and then cancelled in proof a preface for it. 'I call *The Vatican Swindle* a "satirical farce",' he said, or rather refrained from saying, 'just as I called my three preceding works "narratives"[1] in order to make it clear that they are not *novels*. So far I have written nothing but ironical, or if you prefer it, critical works, of which no doubt this is the last.' This *post factum* reclassification of his works has always been a red herring for admirers and a rat-trap for hostile critics. Perhaps in some mystical sense, these last have felt, Gide's earlier novels were not novels at all; then we have only to show that *The Coiners* is not a novel, and we shall have proved that Gide is not a novelist! In fact, of course, *The Immoralist*, *The Vatican Swindle*, and the rest are novels in the accepted sense of the word. Even *André Walter*, despite its diary form, is as much a novel as, say, *Obermann*. The real interest of Gide's paradox lies in his enlarged conception of his vocation. After his re-discovery of Dostoevsky and Stendhal a novel no longer meant, to him, something small and perfect like *Dominique*[2] or *Strait is the Gate*, but something complex and enormous like *La Chartreuse de Parme* or *The Possessed*; and he wished to ensure that his greatest work should be judged on this level.

The Vatican Swindle marked Gide's farewell to the ironical-critical as an art form. But the two elements, of laughter, and

[1] Nevertheless, in the ordinary editions, including the first, both *The Immoralist* and *Strait is the Gate* have the sub-title 'a novel'; and while they were in process of composition Gide invariably referred to them as 'my novel.'

[2] *Strait is the Gate* owes nearly as much, in plot, style, and atmosphere, to Fromentin's *Dominique* as to Gide's own life.

counterpoint between apparent and real meaning, remained permanent in his work; and he never ceased to be ironic in the fuller, Socratic sense. By leaving his intentions inexplicit and immanent, he induced the reader not merely to witness, but to explore and experience the inner significance of his works. It is the difference between pouring water on a duck's back, and injecting a medicament into its veins! Meanwhile, by abandoning his preface, he left *The Vatican Swindle* to the next generation, and allowed contemporary critics to pretend that he advocated the pushing of inoffensive elderly gentlemen out of railway trains.

The novel had found its central incident, and was to reach a burlesque apotheosis, in a railway carriage. On 7 January 1930 Gide was returning by train from Toulon to Paris with Jacques de Lacretelle. At the opposite table, which was covered with flowers, sat a honeymoon couple, the husband engrossed in *The Vatican Swindle*. It was the first time Gide had ever seen a stranger reading *himself*. 'Here's your chance,' said Lacretelle, 'Tell him who you are – write him a dedication!' But to do this, Gide would have had to feel sure that the unknown liked the book. Suddenly the young man pulled out a penknife. Good heavens, was he about, like Lafcadio, to plunge it in his thigh? But no, worse still, he seemed to intend to cut the book itself in pieces, and Lacretelle was seized with a *fou rire*. With great care the bridegroom cut the threads of the binding, detached the part he had read, handed it to his young wife; and both buried themselves in their reading.

7

ARMAGIDON

Turkish March, Numquid et tu . . . ? If It Die . . . ,
Pastoral Symphony, Corydon

'If ye were blind, ye should be without sin.' – John ix, 41.
Quoted in *Pastoral Symphony*.

In April and May 1914 Gide made a journey to Turkey with
Ghéon and Mme Mayrisch, a wealthy patroness of the arts;
characteristically, he left his novel to appear without him. His
journal for the trip appeared in the *NRF* as *La Marche Turque*, a
title which, besides its obvious meaning,[1] embodies one of Gide's
two puns from Beethoven; the reference being to the well-known
Turkish march in the suite 'The Ruins of Athens'. At moments he
had felt on the verge of an ecstasy that would recall Tunisia and
his youth; but the desolation of the country and the hideousness
of the people changed his expectancy to disgust. The time for re-
peal of his renunciation of travel had not yet come. Here and
there he noted, without foreseeing more than another Balkan
conflict, preparations for war. He retreated to Greece, and as he
neared the Piraeus recited to himself Poe's lines 'To Helen'.
'Now I know,' he wrote, 'that our Western (I was about to say
French) civilization is not only the most beautiful; it is the only
one, yes, the very civilization of Greece, of which we are sole
heirs.' This is one of the earliest expressions of the return of his
long-dormant regard for classicism, both Hellenic and French,
which increased during the second half of his life, and culminated
in *Theseus*.

On his return he made a memorandum 'to repeat to myself
every morning that the most important is yet to be said, and that it

---

[1] *Marche* in French can mean either journey or march.

is high time.' He reproached himself for allowing a bout of piano-practice to distract him from his work; but a greater obstacle was on the way. On 28 July he stood on the quay at Dieppe, about to embark for England to join Valéry Larbaud, when the newspaper placards showed the imminence of war. His journey was not to take place for four years. He hurried to Cuverville to provide for his wife's safety; then, having asked her to say the Lord's Prayer beside him ('I did it for her sake, and all my pride yielded pain-lessly to my love'), he went to Paris 'to look for something to do.' How like the autumn of 1939 it seems, to a later generation! There is a thunderstorm like a bombardment; there are long days of exquisite sunlight; and 'the air is full of a loathsome anguish.' 'A writer's duty during a war is to abstain from writing,' Gide remarked to Charles du Bos at this time, and for eighteen months he performed this negative but heroic duty. It was for the young to provide and endure, and the old to organize the suffer-ings of war; the middle-aged could only alleviate them. During August and September he worked for the Red Cross in Paris, and with Jean Schlumberger in a convalescent hospital at Braffy. The German thrust seemed to menace Cuverville. He returned, sent the Drouin, Gilbert, and Copeau women and children to safety, and awaited invasion with his wife, until the enemy attack switched towards Paris and ended in the battle of the Marne. In October he became assistant-director of the Foyer Franco-Belge, a relief organization for Belgian refugees, and worked there, 'devoured by sympathy,' and accompanied by his oldest and lifelong woman friend, Mme Théo van Rysselberghe, until February 1916. Then, excluded by a *coup d'état* in the Foyer, he broke away, exhausted, from the war's unmanageable stupidity, and retired to Cuverville to cultivate his garden. He kept his vow of silence by publishing nothing during the war, but began again to write. His great novel was taking vague shape, and he performed the works that still separated him from it.

On 3 April 1915 Pierre Dupouey, a friend of Gide and a re-cent Catholic convert, had died at the front, leaving letters to his wife of a marvellous religious fervour. His friend's testament of grace reopened in Gide the old wound of Claudel's spear, and in

January 1916 converted Ghéon, Gide's companion in the boulevard prowlings of the late '90s, outright. One night Gide dreamed he was advancing with Ghéon up a narrowing valley, wooded and paradisal, until his friend halted and said, pointing to his rosary: 'No farther: henceforth between us there is *that.*' And next day Gide read the terrible text in St John: 'If a man abide not in me, he is cast forth as a branch and is withered; and men gather them and cast them into the fire, and they are burned.' 'Truly,' he wrote in anguish, 'was I not "cast into the fire", and already a prey to the most abominable desires?' Ghéon's apostasy to faith came when Gide was exhausted by his ministry to the displaced persons of Belgium, sickened by the war, and perhaps in the commencing throes of a strange affair of the heart which we shall have to examine later. Moreover Gide's wife, innocently but most uncharacteristically, opened and read a letter from Ghéon, in which his converted and sanctified friend alluded to the unhallowed joys they had shared so long and until so recently. Had Mme Gide never suspected before then, as Gide believed until after her death in 1938? Or had she known always but remained silent, as he then decided? However this might be, she knew now. In Shakespeare's phrase, he was 'tired with all these' –'Everything in me calls out to be revised, amended, re-educated,' he wrote – and all through 1916 he underwent a moral and religious crisis which was his dark night of the soul. Remorse and self-disgust alternated with periods of calm meditation; mainly for the latter he reserved a special diary which he called *Numquid et tu . . .?*

The words came from John vii: 'Are ye also led astray? . . . Art thou also of Galilee?' – questions which Gide felt, with all they hold and all he added to them of ambiguity, to be addressed personally to himself. Because he replies to all their possible meanings, there is something of the same ambiguity latent beneath the exquisite simplicity of his answers; and Catholicism is made to feel the recoil of every effort he makes towards the purity of the Gospels. 'It is not so much a matter of believing Christ's words because he is Son of God,' he observes, 'as of understanding that he is Son of God because his word is divine.' And when he quotes John vii, 53: 'And each one returned to his house,' he cries: 'Lord!

he who comes to you no longer has a house': it is the truth that
Claudel and the Elder Brother had denied, and the Prodigal had
been too weary to maintain. But *Numquid et tu . . .?* is only inci-
dentally an attack on Catholicism and Claudelism. 'The Gospel is a
simple book, which must be read simply: it is a question not of
explaining it, but of accepting it.' And in return for this humility,
and that of his horror of 'the terrible stain of sin,' he found that the
truths he had discovered in his own life were already announced in
the Gospels. The culmination of individualism in abnegation,
man's duty to be happy, eternity and the Kingdom of Heaven this
side of the grave, 'paradisal fruition of each instant,' all were there.
He gazed through the strait gate, and saw within a truth he could
accept with open eyes, a joy keen as Ghéon's in his blind plunge
into the broad abyss of the Church! And he brought to his brief
book a devout ardour, a beauty of enunciation that could scarcely
be matched in French literature since Pascal.

In June the inevitable movement of retreat set in: the date
coincides with the first important disagreement with his wife recorded in the *Journal*.[1] 'I was happy, you have ruined my happiness, jealous God,' he cries; 'you have poisoned with bitterness all
the springs whereat I quenched my thirst.' His fervour is, after all,
less than in *Fruits of the Earth*. Then he looked to find God round
the next corner, in the next pomegranate: now, face to face with
Him, praying, beseeching, arguing, he is more an individual than
ever. He holds a dialogue with God, but is not merged in Him;
and at the end, fortified by his taste of grace, he is free again. 'My
thought was truest when it was boldest. . . . Why did I not remain
entire and obstinate in my own path!' He published his book only
in 1926, and wrote in the preface: 'I would sign these pages today
with all my heart; but perhaps I would no longer write them.'

It had always been Gide's way to follow, in each of his major
works, a trend opposite to those of the one before and the one
after – to write *Fruits* after *Marshlands, Strait is the Gate* after *The
Immoralist*. But throughout the year of his religious meditations
he was writing two works of opposite polarity simultaneously. In
March 1916, a month after the commencement of *Numquid et*

---

[1] Due to her reading Ghéon's incriminating letter.

tu . . . ? he began his memoirs. Yet this, the story of his emancipation, was also the story of his love for his cousin, the 'mystic orientation' whose centripetal force had enabled him to counterpoise liberty with constraint, prodigality with return. He marked this, the less apparent but not the less important theme of his autobiography, by choosing its title, *Si le grain ne meurt . . . (If It Die . . .)*, from a text he had already expounded in *Numquid et tu . . . ?* 'Except a grain of wheat fall into the ground and die, it abideth alone; but if it die, it bringeth forth much fruit.' Gide's early self had died when he freed himself from his mother and fell ill at Biskra; its death had brought forth much fruit, including *Fruits of the Earth*! And by substituting his cousin for his mother, he took a homeopathic dose of the virtue and duty which had enslaved his boyhood, and thereby brought new integration to his freedom. *If It Die . . .* ends with the death of his mother and his engagement to Madeleine Rondeaux.

Many think that in *If It Die . . .* Gide wrote his finest work; if so, it was unintentional, for his chief purpose was to mark one of several stages in clearing the way for his novel. But his memoirs are, next to Rousseau's *Confessions* and Chateaubriand's *Mémoires d'Outre-Tombe*, the greatest autobiography in the French language. There is little question here of influence, but by affinity Gide's work irresistibly recalls that of his predecessor Rousseau. Both have the delicious charm and health of living waters; though Rousseau's is like the gush of a perennial spring, Gide's is more like the irrigation channels that had enchanted him in the orchards of Biskra. In one mood we may prefer the romantic indiscipline of Rousseau, evolving from sensibility to paranoia, in another the canalized classic beauty of Gide: Rousseau is tremendous, Gide is exquisitely subdued. The qualities of formal charm he deplored and misnamed in this work, when in a moment of despondency he called it 'studied, subtle, dry, elegant, faded',[1] are in fact organically appropriate. Where Rousseau had told his tale up to sinister nightfall, Gide ended at dawn; his theme is the wonder-world of genius in youth: he confessed himself in an idyll.

If It Die . . . is a confession. Rousseau confessed to posterity,

[1] *Journal*, 13 October 1916.

Ghéon to a priest. Gide, like Raskolnikov, told to the market-place of his contemporaries the crime that had made him great. 'I am not writing these memoirs in order to defend myself,' he recorded;[1] 'I am not called upon to defend myself, since I am not accused. I am writing them before being accused. I am writing them in order to be accused.' After *If It Die . . .* and *Corydon* he need no longer feel that he was writing under false pretences; when he came to publish his great novel, the public would know who had written it. And he postponed the release of *If It Die . . .* till 1926, the year of *The Coiners*.

In November 1917 Gide suspended the writing of his memoirs, just before reaching the crucial epoch of his rebirth at Biskra. There was no great urgency, it is true; but his relations with his wife had again reached a difficult stage, and it is possible that he stopped in order to spare her feelings, and from gratitude for her patience. Already in December 1916, when he read her the opening chapters, he felt 'such palpitations of the heart that at moments I was forced to interrupt myself.'

It is an astonishing fact that Gide had planned his next short novel, *Pastoral Symphony*, several years before the occurrence in his life of the events that resemble its plot and inspired its actual writing.[2] He first mentions the novel in his *Journal* for 30 May 1910. It is to be called *The Blind Girl*, and to deal with the opposition of true Christianity to both Catholicism and Protestantism. It was not till January 1916 that Gide seems to have begun, as if living his unwritten novel, a love-affair with Élisabeth, daughter of his old friend Mme Théo van Rysselberghe. A Freudian would not fail to notice that this unconscious choice suggests, like his love for his cousin, the attraction to a sister-image so prevalent in those whose childhood has been dominated by a powerful mother. In December 1916, in the train on the way back from Verhaeren's funeral, he passed her a note to say that he would like to give her a child; but this wish, perhaps merely playful at the time, was to

---

[1] *Journal*, 19 January 1917.
[2] He had even mentioned its basic subject – the blind girl whose blindness is an innocence that frees her from the conventional morality of people with sight – to Paul Laurens before their departure to North Africa in 1893.

Madeleine Gide, 1902 (*Collection Mme Catherine Lambert Gide*)

Gide with Marc Allégret in England, 1918 (*Marc Allégret*)

Gide with his daughter Catherine, Élisabeth van Rysselberghe, Mme Théo van Rysselberghe, and Roger Martin du Gard, 1924 (*Mme Christiane Martin du Gard*)

Gide with Dindiki, Congo, 1926 (*Collection Mme Catherine Lambert Gide*)

Gide leaving for Moscow, 1936 (*Collection M Catherine Lambert Gide*)

wait six years for its fulfilment.[1] Their attachment had begun, like Paolo and Francesca's in Dante, over the reading together of a book; or rather, since the book was Browning, the similarity is more to Pompilia and Caponsacchi in *The Ring and the Book*; and when, on 22 July 1922, Gide read aloud to mother and daughter Pompilia's monologue, he exclaimed in his *Journal*: 'Abnegation can go no farther.' The event contributed, as much as Ghéon's conversion, to the spiritual unrest of the year; in June 1916 it perhaps helped to cause the 'terrible crisis' in his relations with his wife; and all this was reflected, two years later, in his novel, which he began on 16 February 1918 and finished in the following October.

Pastoral Symphony is the diary of a Swiss Protestant minister. He is called to the bedside of a dying old woman, and there finds a fifteen-year-old girl, blind, verminous, and apparently an idiot. She has never learned to speak, and does not understand the speech of others; her face is a mask of hostility and indifference. Feeling that God has 'placed in his way an obligation that it would be cowardly to avoid', he takes her to his home. She is, he tells his wife, the lost sheep of the Gospels, who is more precious than all the rest of the flock. 'Grant, O Lord,' he prays, 'that my love may lighten her terrible darkness.' By 'love' he means 'charity,' and this verbal confusion is the root of the tragedy that follows.

The pastor teaches Gertrude to speak and read, and rejoices in the beauty and joy of the soul he helps her to regain. He takes her to a concert at Neuchâtel where Beethoven's Pastoral Symphony is played. 'Is what you see really as beautiful as that?' she asks, and the pastor, troubled, can only reply, 'Those who have eyes do not know their own happiness.' But all is not harmonious in their own symphony. The pastor's wife is unable to approve what seems to her an excess of charity. 'You do for her what you would not have done for any of your own family,' she says. And when the pastor finds his son is in love with Gertrude, and informs his wife, saying, 'At that age people do not know their own desires,' she answers strangely, 'They don't always know them even when they are older.' On questioning Gertrude he is relieved by her simple

[1] Jean Lambert, *Gide familier*, p. 91.

reply: 'You know it is you I love.' Rebuking Jacques for tampering with her innocence, he sends him away, and for double security lodges Gertrude with a friend.

Gertrude's blindness can be cured by an operation. Before she leaves for hospital, she informs the pastor that their love is carnal; willingly, and sharing her absence of guilt, the poor man succumbs. But Gertrude, her sight restored, falls in love with the handsome face of Jacques; too late, for he has become a Catholic, and means to be a priest. And when she sees the ageing face of the pastor, lined with his uneasy virtue, she tries to drown herself. 'When I saw Jacques I knew it was not you that I loved,' she tells him in their last interview; 'he had your face, I mean the face I imagined you had. Let us part – I cannot bear to see you again'; and that night she dies. 'It would not be fitting for me to accuse you, Father,' says Jacques, 'but I have been guided by the example of your errors.' The pastor begs his wife to pray for him: she obliges by reciting the Lord's Prayer as Mme Gide had done on the outbreak of war in 1914. 'I should have liked to weep, but felt my heart more arid than the desert.'

The very place and time of the action are intimately associated with Gide himself: it was at La Brévine in the '90s that he had finished *Marshlands* and begun *Fruits*; and his impressions of Switzerland had recently been revived by a visit during August 1917, in circumstances still more blissful than the pastor's. Something like the triangle in the pastor's life had occurred in 1916, as we have seen, in Gide's. There is less, however, in the wife's harshness, of the patient and sensitive Madeleine Gide, than of Gide's sisters-in-law; and the instruction of Gertrude recalls Gide's tutoring of his nephews and nieces, of which their mothers had sometimes shown jealousy.[1] *Pastoral Symphony* is, in part, a satire on the dangers of education, which, if taken to the deep spiritual relationship where it can do most good, corrupts both teacher and pupil. The theological controversy between the pastor and his son,

---

[1] It is also modelled on that of Helen Keller, whose autobiography had appeared in French translation in 1916. The original idea had no doubt been suggested in 1893 by the life of the deaf, dumb and blind American girl Laura Bridgman (1829–89), whom Gide mentions in his novel.

Christ against Paul, uses the same texts and arguments as Gide versus Ghéon in *Numquid et tu . . .?* Gide had reached the same conclusion as the pastor, who writes: 'Is it a betrayal of Christ, a diminution or profanation of the Gospel, to see therein primarily a *method for attaining a happy life?*' It is at the next step that they part company – at the discovery that the Devil (in whom Gide was beginning, if only as an indispensable metaphor, to believe) has for some time back been guiding their thoughts. For the pastor it is spiritual bankruptcy; for Gide it is a realization that the Devil, if one has the intelligence to understand him without being his dupe, can be a valuable instructor in ethics and psychology. This is his chief new theme during the decade 1916–26; and *Pastoral Symphony* is a first experiment, controlled and isolated, in the methods and successes of the Devil. The pastor is, like Michel, Lafcadio, and others, only a fragment of Gide's personality, set free to do evil and point a moral where Gide could not follow.

Gide was indignant when the critics saw the pastor as a portrait of himself. 'If I use myself as a model,' he ambiguously explains, 'it is because I have first become the very person I wished to portray.' Yet his unhappy hero is very like a projection of one half of his self-characterization in the *Journal* of 22 June 1907: 'I am a little boy having a good time, combined with a Protestant pastor who bores him.' Perhaps his annoyance would have been less if the pastor had not been taken for a villain and a hypocrite. In fact he is a man whom the Devil tempts, since he has no vices, through his ruling virtue, his charity. There is nothing to show that his love for Gertrude, however possessive, would ever have become physical, if she had not seduced him. Ultimately Gertrude's unconsciousness of evil, of which her blindness is a symbol, is more dangerous spiritually than the pastor's consciousness of virtue. The pastor misapplies to her Christ's word to the Pharisees: 'If ye were blind ye should have no sin'; blind she is an Alissa, seeing she is an Isabelle; at last she is revealed as a kind of witch, and her final words to her victim are of an abominable cruelty and egoism. Nor can the pastor's wife be acquitted of a share in the tragedy. Her desiccated, negative virtue ('the only pleasure she would accept from me was abstinence from things that displeased her,' complains the pastor) is Pharisaic rather than Christian, and her silence, where speech might have saved her husband and her rival, is the vengeance she allows her jealousy. The Devil is, in fact, triumphant all along the line; and though outwardly *Pastoral Symphony* streams with radiance and joy, internally it is the darkest and most terrible of Gide's fictions. Its pessimism is crystallized in the sinister irony of its title. This is the second of Gide's puns from Beethoven. 'Pastoral' is the adjective derived from pastor; and the difference between the two symphonies, Beethoven's and the pastor's, is the difference between innocent blindness and guilty sight.

A still more serious crisis in Gide's marriage than the ominous troubles of 1916 had begun in the year before the commencement of *Pastoral Symphony*, reached its height when the novel was half written, and ended soon after his work was completed in a terrible punishment which the novel itself might seem to have predicted. In May 1917, as Madeleine immediately guessed, began Gide's joyful and lasting friendship for the fifteen-year-old Marc Allégret, son of his former tutor and best man the Protestant pastor Élie Allégret. This infidelity to his wife, as he well knew, was made only the more heinous by the moral and intellectual nobility of his new love, so entirely different from the innumerable brief sensual liberations which had gone before and were to follow after, and which, as it seemed to him, robbed her of nothing.[1] This love wronged his wife not because it was physical, but because it was spiritual: for the first time, as she felt, he had taken back the inalienable gift of his soul. In June 1918 he eloped with Marc Allégret to spend the summer and autumn in England. 'You are not going away alone, are you?' she asked. 'No,' he stammered. 'You are going with Marc?' 'Yes.' 'Don't say anything. Never tell me anything again. I prefer your silence to your dissimulation.' In a desperate effort to explain, which blinded him, like his pastor, to the cruelty of his words, he wrote to her that he must leave

---

[1] 'These frequent impulsive encounters, transient and without sequel, that my nature obliged me incessantly to seek, could not in any way affect or change the integrity of my surrender to her of my whole heart,' Gide told Roger Martin du Gard in 1920.

because he was 'rotting away' at Cuverville; and she, momentarily more generous than the pastor's wife, wrote in return to release him: 'I have had the best part of your soul, the affection of your boyhood and youth. And I know that, alive or dead, I shall have the soul of your old age.' So it was to be. But when he finished *Pastoral Symphony* at Cambridge on 18 October the fatal and innocent blind girl had become an expression not only of Élisabeth van Rysselberghe but also of Marc Allégret. And the end of the novel foretold the disaster that awaited him at Cuverville; for the tragedy of *Pastoral Symphony* is not the death of Gertrude, but the death of the pastor's wife's love for her husband.

Soon after his return he began to work again on *If It Die . . .*, and asked his wife for the letters he had written to her in their youth and during his many absences since their marriage. She had burned them all. 'I read every one before destroying them,' she said, 'they were my dearest possession on earth.' Gide's sins against her had been heavy indeed, but were exactly balanced by this merciless and final revenge. Gide was stricken (and has been callously blamed for it) by the loss of what seemed to him the noblest and purest of his works, of an indispensable source for his autobiography, which would now end for ever at the moment of their betrothal. But his grief, above all, was for her denial of his love and withdrawal of her own. Their mutual love was the profoundest truth of his life and hers; it continued to exist, consciously for him, unconsciously in her; and the estrangement caused by her symbolic act of murder and suicide was the more tragic for being onesided and false. If we wish to judge this human drama equitably we must remember that the egoism and frailty of it were not unilateral, that Mme Gide requited the anguish she had suffered in full and in her own coin.

Gide called *Pastoral Symphony* 'my last debt to the past'; but two more works were still required to clear the way for his great novel. He finished *If It Die . . .* early in 1919, and *Corydon* was already completed. He had tried to read both these to his wife. 'It isn't the book you think it is,' he mistakenly assured her of *Corydon*; but soon he said: 'I haven't the strength to continue,' and she replied: 'I think it would be useless.' Half of *Corydon*, it is true, had been written in the summer of 1910, and printed, privately, anonymously, and in an edition of twelve copies, in the following year; but it was only in December 1917 that Gide resumed his work. It was completed in June 1918, again privately printed in 1920, and released at last to the public in 1924. The delay was persuaded by Marcel Drouin, who saw in the book the sign of an obsession, and a menace to his brother-in-law's career; on the contrary, Gide affirms, it deals with a problem that no longer troubles him, because he has found a practical solution, and 'I value nothing of which my book will deprive me.' The quotation from Ibsen in the preface: 'Friends are dangerous not so much in what they make us do, as in what they prevent us from doing' is to Drouin's address.

The title alone would be sufficient to announce the subject of *Corydon* to a Frenchman. In English pastoral Corydon is un-classically matched with a shepherdess; in France the name is almost a technical term, and the reference to the first line of Virgil's Second Eclogue is well understood: 'For fair Alexis shepherd Corydon burned.' *Corydon* is a treatise on the legitimacy, salubrity, and expediency of homosexuality.

The narrator, a militant heterosexual (because he calls himself 'I' the unwary reader might mistake him for Gide himself), has been perturbed by the Eulenburg scandal of 1907, and calls on Corydon, a doctor of medicine and a homosexual, out of an impartial desire to hear the other side. Corydon, providentially, is writing a book on the subject, the substance of which he argues with his friend in four highly Socratic dialogues on four successive days. He demonstrates that what is conventionally called 'unnatural vice' is both natural and a virtue. From entomology, biology and zoology he constructs a Darwinian theory of the evolutionary necessity of homosexuality. From sociology he shows that the lamentable prevalence of heterosexuality is chiefly due to the warping forces of education and conformism, and that homosexuals make excellent husbands and fathers. As La Rochefoucauld says: 'How many men would ever have experienced love if they had never heard talk of it?' Lastly he goes to history to prove that the epochs of uranism, classical Greece and the Renaissance, were the healthiest in art and morality; and that the exclusive love of women is a morbid symptom of decadence in art, state and the family. Fortunately the fifth day, on which Corydon, one feels, might have advocated long sentences in Reading Gaol for the average man, never comes. His questioner retires, 'convinced that to certain affirmations a prudent silence is a better answer than any words one could find'.

As a critic of Gide has remarked,[1] 'it is not very convincing.' Fortunately, Gide's book is more impressive in the reading than in the summary, and his presentation of the evidence is brilliantly superior to his conclusions. 'I mean not to raise pity, but to arouse misgivings,' he said, and if he had been content with the production of disquieting ideas, *Corydon* would have been a better book. As it is, he proves not only the normality of uranism but the abnormality of heterosexuality; a society founded on *Corydon* would substitute proscription of heterosexuals for the equally deplorable present proscription of homosexuals.

In later years Gide regretted, surely mistakenly, the element of irony in *Corydon*. *Corydon* unites two favourite forms of Gide, the *sotie* and the 'imaginary interview'. Like all the works he called 'critical', Gide's book is, intentionally, comic as well as serious. Outworn conventions, he knew, are based on irrational taboos, and taboos are best overthrown not by reasoned argument, but by raising the stakes, by using satirical overstatement to goad the reader into thinking for himself. English readers may perhaps best appreciate the ironic method of *Corydon* by comparing it with a classic of their own, a novel which proves, with a similar outrageousness, that crime is a disease and disease a crime, that religion tends to be a form of banking and banking a form of religion, and that machines are alive and mean to destroy the human race. As a satire *Corydon* is analogous to Samuel Butler's *Erewhon*. Its irony, rather than its morally admirable sincerity and courage, makes it more than a treatise in propaganda and amateur science, gives it wit, formal beauty and level upon level of meaning, and saves it as a work of art. By its irony it ranks not with *Return from the U S S R,* but with *Marshlands.*

[1] Paul Archambault in *Humanité d'André Gide.*

8

'MY FIRST NOVEL'

The Coiners, Dostoevsky, Journal of 'The Coiners'

'We are all bastards.' – *Cymbeline*, Act ii, scene 5.

The way was now at last cleared for the writing of *The Coiners*
By a deliberate gamble with fate and advancing age Gide had
completed his programme, had written everything else first. 'The
enormity of the shapeless material oppresses me,' he had written in
1915, 'I don't know how to take hold of it, or how to come
through, or whether I shall have the strength.' Between 17 June
1919, when he began the active incubation of his novel, and 8
June 1925, when he wrote its last words, lay the immense labour of
six years. It was not till November 1921 that he reached the first
pages. Two and a half years had been spent in wrestling with a
work that insisted on progressively enlarging itself; like a hydra, it
had many heads. In it all the ideas Gide had fought or made his
own were presented, and brought to a dialectic equilibrium, by
embodiment in nearly all the people he had importantly loved,
opposed, and observed. It was, as his hero claimed, a 'crossroads of
problems': it was also a crossroads of characters. It is the union of
tension and ease, of enormous diversity with exquisite grace and
harmony, that makes *The Coiners* one of the world's greatest
novels: shall we say, since some such estimate has to be made,
tacitly or not, on every major work of art, that *The Coiners*
should come last in any list of the first ten[1] – and that in formal
beauty, if not in energy, it is surpassed by none of the preceding
nine?

[1] For example: *Bouvard et Pécuchet, The Possessed, A la Recherche du Temps Perdu,
War and Peace, La Chartreuse de Parme, Wuthering Heights, Moby Dick, Finnegans
Wake, Eugene Onegin, The Coiners*. The eleventh? *Our Mutual Friend*.

On a suffocating summer evening, when all his family are out, Bernard Profitendieu discovers some old love-letters of his mother's, which show that he is her bastard by a former lover. He writes a calculatedly insulting letter to his foster-father, and leaves home, spending the night with his school-friend Olivier Molinier. Olivier's younger brother Georges overhears their conversation.

Olivier's elder brother Vincent is regretting a love-affair with Laura Douviers, née Vedel, who is with child by him. Led astray by Robert de Passavant, a wealthy dilettante, who wishes to use him to become better acquainted with Olivier, he deserts Laura and becomes the lover of Lady Lilian Griffith.

Olivier's Uncle Édouard, a novelist, is summoned from England by a pitiful appeal from Laura, his former pupil and platonic beloved. Like Passavant, he is attracted by Olivier – the card he has sent his half-sister Pauline, Olivier's mother, giving the time of his arrival, is meant for Olivier's eyes. Olivier duly comes to the station, but each hides his joy at the meeting too successfully, and mistakes the other's embarrassment for indifference. Édouard distractedly throws away his left-luggage receipt, which is picked up by Bernard, who redeems the suitcase, finding in it money for lunch and Édouard's diary.

Édouard, Bernard reads, having long severed relations with Pauline, had never seen his nephews: until, last autumn, he found a schoolboy stealing a book from a stall, and discovered his name to be Georges Molinier. Intrigued, he immediately called on Pauline, and so met Olivier. They saw each other again, on the occasion of Laura's wedding to Douviers, a worthy professor of French at Cambridge. Laura's father keeps a school, where Olivier and Georges are half-boarders. Édouard, distressed that Laura's brother Armand encourages his sister Sarah to flirt with Olivier, despondently left for England. Next in the dossier comes Laura's letter; and Bernard, following his motto, 'If you don't, who will?' calls on her at the address it gives, falls in love, and offers his assistance. Surprised by the amused Édouard, the resourceful youth suggests himself as the novelist's secretary. Édouard visits his sister, hoping to see Olivier; but Olivier that evening is with Passavant.

Abandoning hope of Olivier, Édouard takes Bernard and Laura to Saas-Fé in Switzerland, where he has been asked by his old piano-teacher, La Pérouse, to keep an eye on young Boris, bastard child of the old man's dead son. Olivier, thinking himself scorned, takes appropriate revenge by going to Corsica with Passavant, as *his* secretary.

Édouard is writing a novel called '*The Coiners*'! He is 'allowing reality to dictate it': its theme is 'the conflict between actual and artistic reality'. In perhaps the most painful scene of Gide's novel, Édouard explains the imaginary '*Coiners*' to Bernard, Laura, and Mme Sophroniska[1] (Boris's psychoanalyst); they are baffled and bored; and the most clinching criticism comes from Bernard, who, like Lafcadio foxing Julius with a real gratuitous act, produces a 'real' spurious ten-franc piece, which has been passed upon him that very morning. At the end of summer Laura returns to her forgiving husband, while Bernard and La Pérouse become ushers, and little Boris a boarder, at the Vedel Pension.

Young Georges has been leader of a gang of schoolboys who visited a brothel after school. They do not know that it is Bernard's foster-father, Judge Profitendieu, who has had their resort tactfully raided during the vacation, having discovered that the son of his colleague Molinier is involved. Georges is now ripe for worse. The formidable Strouvilhou, friend of Passavant and an old boy of the Pension Vedel, employs a young cousin, Ghéridanisol, Georges' school-fellow, to organize the boys to circulate his bogus ten-franc pieces.

Olivier is to be editor of Passavant's new literary review, and invites Édouard and Bernard to a reception in honour of the opening number. For the first time he sees the virtue of his beloved uncle confronted with the mediocrity of his false new friends. Weeping with grief and shame, he says to Édouard, 'Take me away.' Armand succeeds in arranging for his sister Sarah to spend the night with Bernard.

Next day Olivier attempts suicide, and is nursed back to life

---

[1] An eminent pupil of Freud named Mme Sokolnicka held weekly meetings, attended by Gide and the *NRF* group, in Paris in 1921. See George Gabory's *Essai sur Marcel Proust*, pp. 25–35.

by Édouard; thenceforth the course of their love will be tranquil. Édouard receives visits from Pauline, who resigns Olivier to his care – and from Profitendieu, who begs him to intercede with Bernard to return home. Both ask him to warn young Georges, whose connection with the forged money is known to Profitendieu. Édouard sees Passavant, who pretends to be delighted to be rid of Olivier. Passavant receives Strouvilhou, who explains his policy of saving mankind by destruction of the weak.

Bernard is awarded his baccalaureate with distinction. All day he disputes, and all night he wrestles, with an angel. 'The time has come to settle your accounts,' says the divine being. He sleeps no more with Sarah, leaves the Pension Vedel, and decides to live by rule – but what rule? Édouard gives him the formula; 'One must follow one's bent – so long as it is upward.'

Édouard's novel has a passage where the novelist hero warns a boy resembling Georges, by showing him a passage in *his* novel where the lamentable morality and probable fate of a similar boy are discussed. Édouard in turn warns Georges by showing him this chapter. Georges' reaction is delight at Édouard's finding him sufficiently interesting to put him in his novel.

Armand, who has replaced Olivier as editor of Passavant's review, shows his friend a letter from a brother in Africa, describing a meeting with a man who, after murdering his mistress, believes himself to be the Devil. Neither recognizes the mad assassin as Vincent, his victim as Lady Griffith.

Ghéridanisol passes Georges' warning to Strouvilhou, and the traffic in forged pieces is stopped. He and Georges persuade little Boris to undertake a test of courage: he is to shoot himself in class with a pistol that Ghéridanisol has stolen from La Pérouse, and knows to be loaded, though he tells Georges it is not. Boris blows out his brains before his grandfather's eyes. Georges is horrified into reforming, Bernard returns to his father, Édouard decides not to use the death of Boris (he believes it to be suicide) for his novel. Invited to dinner by Profitendieu, he is pleased by the prospect of meeting Bernard's younger brother, Caloub.

The Coiners is over, leaving us doubtful whether Édouard's 'Coiners' will ever be finished. Édouard's novel is like a fossil ancestor of Gide's, as to whose evolution much other evidence is available. Édouard kept a journal containing 'the continuous critique of my novel.' 'What would we give,' he cries enthusiastically to Laura and Bernard, 'for the journal of *L'Éducation Sentimentale* or *The Brothers Karamazov*! the history of the work, of its gestation!' Gide, too, kept such a journal; and it is perhaps the most detailed account in all literature of the composition of a major novel. But the *Journal of 'The Coiners'* reveals less about what the novel is, than about what it ceased to be; it enhances the value of what Gide retained, by the revelation of what he progressively rejected.

At the end of *Crime and Punishment* Dostoevsky speaks of the future 'slow progressive regeneration' of Raskolnikov, and says, 'this may well form the theme of a new tale'. *The Vatican Swindle* ends with a similar half-promise of a sequel, and as late as August 1921 Gide still intended his novel to be the story of Lafcadio's future; not of his regeneration, for Lafcadio's was essentially a crime without punishment, but of his maturing under the tutelage of Édouard; and in its earliest form the whole tale was to be told through Lafcadio's journal. But other themes and other characters crowded in, and refused to be dwarfed by Lafcadio. A new technical problem insisted on being presented and solved, and became one of the novel's chief virtuosities: the major characters (who far outnumber the minor characters) were to be equal to one another in 'quality', and therefore in reality. Instead of gravitating round a massive central body, they were to revolve in a relatively free ellipse whose foci were Édouard and Passavant. For the sake of equilibrium and proportion the superhuman Lafcadio had to be scaled down to the human Bernard; even so, Bernard still trails subdued clouds of glory that are relics of the immortal Lafcadio.

Édouard and Passavant underwent a similar diminution. Passavant, known at first as 'the Seducer', was to have been the Devil's chief representative in the novel, and to have endeavoured to corrupt the entire family of Pastor Vedel, of which the Molinier boys at this period formed part. But Strouvilhou and Ghéridanisol took over many of his functions, and in the finished novel Passavant is more a comic than an evil figure; his vanity often, as when he disdains to punish Édouard for capturing Olivier, makes him verge on the amiable. Still more striking is the devaluation of Édouard. The action of the novel was to have been a projection of his mind; he becomes in fact himself a projection of the action. It was he, at first, who pointed out to Bernard the counterfeit piece that Bernard (then still called Lafcadio) had failed to notice; in the novel as we have it both the ten-franc piece and the death of Boris are beyond his comprehension – he rejects them from his novel, for which they are too real. With cruel irony Gide makes the chapter of Édouard's *'Coiners'* as read to Georges the only piece of inferior writing in his own, Gide's, novel; and the names of Édouard's characters, Audibert and Eudolfe, revert to the preposterous Maeterlinckians of *The Voyage of Urien*. Gide felt he was most manifestly differentiating Édouard from himself when he made him say: 'I don't know how to invent'; hence his annoyance when the critics absurdly deduced that Gide himself had somehow shown in this and, retrospectively, in his previous novels, a lack of invention. Vincent, too, was a more central figure in the earlier versions. It was the rise of Georges, La Pérouse, the Devil, and most of all Olivier, that necessitated the remodelling of the novel. Olivier, the delightful and malleable Olivier, could never have co-existed with Lafcadio.

The sources of *The Coiners* may be classified as literary, historical, and personal. Dickens, who has rarely been given his due for the idea of unprecedented complexity of plot which he exploited in his last period, was Gide's favourite author, as early as 1894, for 'reading at the end of the day, after a long walk in the woods, in the big green arm-chair at La Roque'. On 24 March 1916 he bought a parcel of Dickens translations; in December 1924 he re-reads *Our Mutual Friend*, 'which helps me to judge *The Coiners*'. More than any other novel, *The Coiners* achieves the transcendent but economical intricacy of plot towards which Dickens, uneconomically to the last, was moving. Moreover Gide's concept of the counterfeit in ideas and persons is closely related to Dickens's concept of 'great expectations.' Gide's passion for Browning was at its height in the early 1920s; the influence of *The Ring and the Book* is still visible in his stereoscopic presentation of events through the eyes of different characters, a device he had originally meant to use yet more extensively. Style and mood, as in *The Vatican Swindle*, resemble Stendhal, but with deeper undertones of Dostoevsky, on whom Gide delivered a series of lectures in February–March 1922. 'I presented my own ethic under cover of Dostoevsky,' he says, but conversely, 'had I never met with Dostoevsky, Nietzsche, Blake, or Browning, I cannot believe that my work would have been different.' In Dostoevsky Gide found nothing that was not already his own; it was the sense in which he had defined 'influence' in *Pretexts*.[1] This fellow-feeling, particularly in the ideas of crime as a gratuitous act, and abnegation as the highest form of individuality and freedom, makes Gide's *Dostoevsky* not a distortion, but the most profoundly authoritative of all studies of its subject. *The Coiners* is Gide's *The Possessed*; though the band of schoolboys recalls *The Brothers Karamazov*, and Bernard's personal duel with the angel corresponds to Ivan Karamazov's with the Devil.

Gide, like Dostoevsky, was sensitive to the mystery that sometimes looms behind a newspaper paragraph. The gang of counterfeiters ('not "gang", sir,' said the ringleader to' the judge, 'say rather "literary club"') actually existed and was broken up in 1906; the suicide of Boris actually took place in a school at Clermont-Ferrand in 1909; and Gide ironically gives newspaper-cuttings as documentation of these strange truths in the *Journal of 'The Coiners'*. On 2 May 1921 he caught a schoolboy stealing from a bookstall. . . .

But the characters are, almost without exception, drawn from the three generations of Gide's personal life – the '80s, the 1900s, and the 1920s – his boyhood, manhood, and middle age. The peopling of the novel was conditioned by the writing of *If It*

---

[1] And, of course, the sense in which I should wish it to be understood, whenever I speak of a writer's influence on Gide, or indeed of Gide's adaptation of a character or incident from real life.

Die . . ., with its stimulation of creative memory. La Pérouse was Gide's old piano-teacher, Marc de la Nux, though the interviews with him come from the *Journal* of 1902–14. Little Boris was a fragile Russian infant at school with Gide in 1879; but he was also de la Nux's grandson Pierre, who in 1902 had to be removed from the École Alsacienne ('because he was too easily head of the class,' Mme de la Nux mendaciously told Gide), and later became secretary to Gide and to the *NRF*. Armand Vedel appears in *If It Die* . . . as son of the unctuous Pastor Bavretel; he has sisters like Rachel and Sarah, and an older brother, a medical student, like Vincent.[1] Into Vincent, however, something has entered of Gide's cousin Paul and of Paul's love-affair with the actress Ventura;[2] though Lady Lilian Griffith owes her Christian name, at least, to Lady Rothermere, who in 1917, with the help of her protégé Paul Méral, translated Gide's *Prometheus*. Georges, or at least his warning, may have been suggested by Gide's nephew K., in whose view in July 1914 he accidentally left a notebook containing 'rather sombre reflections' on K.'s character.[3] But the most important events of Gide's life that appear in the novel, are those associated with Laura and Olivier. In July 1922 Gide's love-affair of 1916 was resumed, again over the reading of Browning, and in January 1923 Catherine, Gide's only child, was born. And in May 1917, as we have seen, began Gide's joyful and lasting friendship with Marc Allégret, son of Gide's former tutor and best man, then aged fifteen. They visited Saas-Fé in Switzerland that August. In December 1917 he was worried for a time by Marc's association with Cocteau. Count Robert de Passavant, though he has elements of Jean Lorrain (a forgotten Cocteau of the 1890s), and, still more, of Count Robert de Montesquiou, chief original of Proust's Charlus, is a banalized version of the seemingly meretricious but in fact genuinely golden genius of Cocteau. His name puns, according to the manner in which one divides its syllables, on the ideas of

[1] Vincent in early versions of the novel was a Vedel, not a Molinier.

[2] Reference to newspapers of the period shows that this was her real name, or at any rate her real stage-name.

[3] There seems insufficient evidence in the *Journal* to show whether K. was Jacques or Dominique Drouin, or a son of Pierre Espinas, husband of Charles Gide's daughter Jeanne.

superficiality and opportunism;[1] his novel, *La Barre fixe,* suggests
Cocteau's *Le Grand Écart*; and the Ghérida- in Ghéridanisol is,
phonetically, an anagram of Radiguet, the gifted boy whose
untimely death in 1923 left Cocteau a *veuf sur le toit*.[2] The evening
of 6 December 1917, when Marc Allégret returned late from a visit
to Cocteau, and the next morning – 'for the first time in my life I
knew the torment of jealousy' – when Cocteau good-naturedly
reassured Gide by repeating their innocent conversation word for
word, were among the central incidents of his novel. Thirty-two
years later, in 1949, the old enemies forgave one another: 'I wanted
to kill you,' Gide confessed. He had been sedulously unkind to
Cocteau in his *Journal* ever since, but Cocteau was more generous.
'He teased me and liked me,' he wrote after Gide's death, and
summed up in words that do honour both to his magnanimity and
to his insight: 'When the reckoning is over, although our figures
are so different, they reach the same total.'

'It is not in offering a solution of certain problems that I can
render a real service to my reader,' Gide wrote in the *Journal of
'The Coiners'*, 'but in forcing him to meditate himself on these
problems, of which I do not admit the possibility of any solution
that is not individual and personal.' One of the problems Gide
sets his reader is the enigma of his title. Who are the 'Coiners'? As
we read the novel, we find the characters falling into groups, each
of which in one way or another is in the coining business; and the
gang who are 'coiners' in the literal sense are only a symbol of
the others. There is the gang of schoolboys, who counterfeit, all
too successfully, a love of evil which they do not feel, the gang of

---

[1] *Pass-avant* suggests 'get-ahead', pas-*savant* 'silly-clever'. Yet another allusion is
more recondite. Passavant is associated with the 'Argonauts', a literary group who
take their name from the Greek heroes who rowed in the first ship; and the leading
man on an oar in the French galleys of the seventeenth century was known as the
passe-avant! Passavant ('Press onward') is also, as Justin O'Brien has pointed out, the
ancestral war cry of Proust's Baron de Charlus (*A la Recherche*, ed. Pléiade, I 754.)
Les Argonautes was in fact the title of a short-lived *avant-garde* literary magazine in
pre-war Paris.

[2] Among the minor characters, Dhurmer suggests Camille Mauclair, the timid
Lucien is Christian Beck (a Belgian poet whom Gide knew in the '90s), Jarry is Jarry
himself. The Argonauts suggest the group of the *Mercure de France*, chief rival of
the N R F, led by Alfred Vallette and his wife Rachilde.

Gide with Mme Théo van Rysselberghe, 1939 (*Mme Gisèle Freund*)

Gide with his daughter, Catherine Lambert, 1947 (*Collection Mme Catherine Lambert Gide*)

Gide with François Mauriac, 1949 (*Mme François Mauriac*)

Gide in his library, Rue Vaneau, 1950 (*Daniel Filipacchi*)

parents who counterfeit for their children's benefit a conventional morality which they do not themselves follow, the gang of writers who counterfeit a literary renaissance, the lovers who counterfeit love. Édouard the novelist is the biggest counterfeiter of all, for he is coining a novel which is a parody of Gide's own, and misses every important factor in the events on which it is based. Gide's novel alone is no fabrication: it rings true.

The Coiners has been called tragic, pessimistic, despairing, cruel. It has its quota, like life itself, of unhappy families, crime, and violent death; but the element of tragedy is dominated by the courage and gaiety of the heroes – it is one of the few novels in which the intellectual activity of the characters is as important as their emotions or their deeds – and the whole novel is alive with Gide's own ironic but heartfelt joy in life. If Gide's plot is Dostoevskian, his style, mood, and outlook have something of the gaiety of Stendhal. It was by the standard of Dostoevsky and Stendhal in the past that he wished to be judged; but by what standard did he wish to be judged in the present? There is an entry in the *Journal of 'The Coiners'* which supplies a significant answer to this question. On 15 March 1923 Gide records a remarkable dream. He was sitting in conversation with Marcel Proust (who had died in the previous November) in Proust's study; he found himself holding a string which was attached to two of the volumes in Proust's bookcase; seized with an irresistible impulse, he pulled the string, and so ruined a magnificently bound edition of Saint-Simon's *Memoirs*! Proust cut short his apologies, with 'an exquisite and lordly affability,' and disappeared; and Gide awoke in the act of sobbing on the bosom of Proust's man-servant, and confessing that his destructive act had been intentional

It would be easy to analyse this dream by Freudian principles – to show that both Proust and the servant are images of Gide's long-dead father, and to reconstruct the unknown childhood crime which the dream reveals and conceals. But there is also a school of analysts who believe every dream to be not only a search for time lost, but an attempt to cope, at a deeper level inaccessible to our waking life, with the problems of the present. Inner necessity and the tricks of fate had made Gide's attitude to Proust profoundly ambivalent. In 1912 Proust, then thought of as an obscure dilettante, had submitted the first section of his immense novel to Gide's publishers, the *NRF*, and Gide had been partly responsible for its rejection. Then the tables were turned, and Gide became converted to a belief in Proust's genius. 'The rejection of your novel will be one of the keenest regrets and remorses of my life,' he wrote to Proust in January 1914; and Proust replied, with the lordly affability of the dream: 'My joy in having your letter infinitely surpasses the joy I would have felt in being published by the *NRF*.' And in 1916 Proust migrated with his novel to the *NRF*.

In November 1922, three months before Gide's dream, Proust had died in a blaze of glory. His novel was already certain of survival, Gide's was only just begun. Would he be able to topple Proust's novel, which, as his dream slyly hints, owed so much to the *Memoirs* of Saint-Simon, from its place in the bookshelf of immortality? But the thread which linked Gide and Proust pulled both ways. The likenesses between *A la Recherche du Temps Perdu* and *The Coiners* are less striking than the differences; but the likenesses exist. Gide's novel has its own Baron de Charlus, its band of adolescents, its preoccupation with the cities of the plain. In both works the chief character is writing a novel that turns out to be, more or less, the very novel we are reading. But the most important resemblance is, that each was written with the conscious intention of writing a great novel. Gide was attempting to rival Proust on his own ground. In the dream the element of jealousy in Gide's attitude towards Proust is brought to a head, confessed, and reconciled. Henceforth, though rivals, they are also colleagues. As for the differences between the two novels, there is none more significant than the status of their heroes; Gide's Édouard is far more rigorously distinct from his creator than Proust's Narrator. The intention of *The Coiners* is not to pass coin, however genuine, of Gide's making, but to enable the reader to achieve independence by minting his own.

SPEAKING OF OTHERS

Journey to the Congo, Return from Lake Chad,
The School for Wives, Robert, Geneviève,
The Redureau Case, The Prisoner of Poitiers, Oedipus,
Persephone, Later Fruits of the Earth,
Back from the USSR, After-thoughts on the USSR.

'I resembled those creatures that cannot grow without successive metamorphoses.' – *Journal*, 8 December 1929.

Towards the end of the writing of *The Coiners* Gide felt himself ready for a new break with past and present. He had reached the climacteric of his life – he was now fifty-five – and needed some great adventure of liberation and joy, some revelation comparable to the lost magic of Tunisia, to tide him over into old age with hope and fertility intact. The air of France was becoming unbreathable: the calumnies of the Catholic critic, Henri Massis, who regarded Gide as the godless corrupter of the post-war generation, the campaign of Henri Béraud (which Béraud called 'the Crusade against the Long Faces') against Gide and the NRF,[1] were at their noisy height. He felt, too, the old urge to disappear before the launching of a major work; and *The Coiners* and *If It Die . . .* demanded a more spectacular vanishing than ever before. In December 1924 – it reminds one, more grimly, of his moustache-shaving after *Strait is the Gate* – he had his appendix removed; in April 1925 he ruthlessly sold his collection of presentation copies

---

[1] Gide sent Béraud a box of chocolates, with the message, 'No, I am not incapable of gratitude, my intimates have lied to you.' Béraud, the arch-patriot, was later to do time for collaboration.

of the works of past friends – notably Louÿs, Régnier[1] and Jammes; and on 14 July 1925 he sailed for the Congo with Marc Allégret. 'What are you going out there to look for?' a passenger inquired, and he replied, 'I am waiting till I am out there to find out.'

Their boat coasted from Dakar to the Congo; they ascended the Congo and Oubangui by river-steamer, motored through the Oubangui district, and marched with a file of native bearers to Lake Chad to meet Gide's friend, Marcel de Coppet, newly appointed Governor of the Chad region. They returned ('every day now brings me nearer Cuverville') by whale-boat down the Logone river, and on foot again through the Cameroon, reaching the coast at Douala in May 1926. Marc Allégret, who in the '30s was to create the exquisite and haunting *Lac aux Dames,* had profited from the trip by making an excellent film of scenery and native life; and in 1927 and 1928 Gide published, in *Journey to the Congo* and *Return from Lake Chad,* his diary of their journey.

The two books, which are really one, are the longest of Gide's works next to the *Journal*; and they have a charm of form and mood which wins them a high and central place in his canon. They were written from day to day, so that the total effect could not have been consciously foreseen; and Gide abstained after his return from any rewriting, lest their spontaneity should be impaired. But his 'shaping spirit of imagination' arranged the daily fortuities of travel into symphonic form. The mode is the 'diverse monotony' of *Amyntas,* though the mood is now not of regret, but of joy set free and keen serenity.

The monotonies, modulating one into the other, are those of the accidental epochs of the journey: motor, march, whale-boat, litter, horseback – forest, savannah, river, rocky hills – tepid autumn, cold nights, appalling heat, the beginning of the rains. Each monotony is composed of detailed diversities: flowers, trees, butterflies, big game; the ailments, miseries, joy, gratitude of the bearers; village dances, receptions by chiefs and sultans, culminating in the comic ballet of Rei Bouba's welcome. Other themes run throughout: the quest, baffled till the last day but one, for the

---

[1] Régnier's witty reaction was to send Gide a copy of his latest novel, inscribed: 'For your next sale'.

primeval forest ('I expected more gloom, more mystery and strangeness'); the history of their boy servants Adoum and Outhman, who form a kind of doublet of the vanished Athman of thirty years before; or the tragedy of Dindiki, Gide's pet potto sloth.[1] There is a charming photograph of Marc, young, slim and eager, and Gide, benign, alert, and contented, sitting at their breakfast-table near a native hut. Both wear solar topees; round Gide's ankle is tied a cord, tracing which one discovers at the end the almost imperceptible Dindiki. The 'perodictic potto' rode for hundreds of miles on Gide's shoulder. He suffered from constipation; Gide administered oil enemas, and tried in vain to discover the unknown article of diet that would have saved him. When he died, Gide knew, he says, the sorrow of a bereaved parent. There are memories of La Roque, painful thoughts of Madeleine Gide, severed in space and spirit, wryly witty shots at his enemies – Marc bags a wild pig, and 'it was as ponderous as a Béraud'. The return journey has a dramatic understructure. Illness on the Logone, mounting heat in the Cameroon imply coming disaster; until rains and journey's end relax the tension. The customary lamentations of equatorial travellers are strangely absent.

The amazed enchantment whose loss he had mourned in *Amyntas* had returned. 'Sometimes there is so light, so gentle and voluptuously sweet a waft of air, that one seems to be breathing well-being'; 'a confused adoration streams from my heart.' Such sentences, taken from the beginning and end of the journey, might have come from *Fruits of the Earth*; but their context is the calm and self-possession by which alone the gospel of *Fruits* could be made permanent. The Congo for Gide was paradise regained – it was never for long to be re-lost.

The Congo had given Gide repossession of his joy in life; it also rekindled in him a sense of social injustice which was to dominate his next decade. He treated the natives as friends, and was rewarded with gratitude and devotion. From the car he would wave to the negroes he passed; at first they would be frightened, and then, as they realized that his gestures were meant in kindness, there

[1] A lemuroid sub-primate, and nothing to do with the edentate sloth of South America.

would be 'cries, yells, stamping of feet, a delirium of astonishment and joy that the white traveller should be willing to notice their advances, should respond to them with cordiality'. Everywhere he saw, with rising compunction and anger, the reasons for their astonishment. French Equatorial Africa was exploited by the so-called 'great concessionary companies'. Hideous atrocities were committed on the natives when they brought in insufficient quantities of the rubber for which they must abandon their food crops, and yet receive derisory payment. 'What demon brought me to Africa?' Gide cried. 'I was at peace: and now I know, and I must speak.' And he foresaw with resolute despair a time when he could no longer 'speak without caring whether anyone listens, write for the readers of tomorrow', but must emulate 'the journalist whose voice carries immediately, at the cost of instant extinction'.

Gide's campaign produced more hubbub than immediate result. A leading article in the *Débats* was perfidiously entitled 'The Exploitation of an Accusation', and the Minister for the Colonies announced that everything would be put right in time. But the eloquence of his accusation of colonial capitalism, of 'the abominable crime of repelling and preventing love', is permanent; permanent, too, though evidently perilous, is the beauty of his example in sacrificing his free art to his constraining conscience. He had made a first step on the way he was to follow until the Second World War. 'An immense plaint inhabits me'; 'no longer merely to advance, but to direct oneself towards an end. ... Inexpressible satisfaction!' But another five years were to elapse before his conversion to communism in the 1930s.

Before a fresh leap, he made his characteristic recoil. Just as, in the tropical luxuriance of the Congo, he had read, by way of contrast, Bossuet and Racine, so now he approached a topic as foreign as possible to his late and future preoccupations. As early as 16 July 1914, he had noted in his *Journal* 'a fine subject for a novel': a girl marries, against her parents' wishes, a man in whom she sees splendid qualities which to them are invisible; then her parents come to admire her husband, while she has discovered, and must now conceal, that he is a hollow fraud. Later he intended

to incorporate the theme in *The Coiners*; it was extruded by the
pressure of the rest, but traces of it are visible in the long-suffering
Pauline Molinier. Between December 1926 and October 1928 he
wrote his novel *L'École des femmes* (*The School for Wives*), ironically
borrowing the title from Molière's play.

Éveline is engaged to Robert. They have promised each to keep
a journal of the early days of their love; and her first disillusion is
when she learns that her lover, so sincere, modest, idealistic, tactful,
and courteous, has not kept his promise. Twenty years later, in
1914, she resumes her journal. Life with a husband who is stuffed
with fine phrases, yet acts only from expediency, has become
intolerable. 'I am the wife of a puppet,'[1] she says – 'Robert is not a
hypocrite; he really believes he feels the sentiments he expresses.'
The family priest tells her that her discontent is caused by pride,
and urges her to submit; but she finds that the humiliation of
submission creates not humility, but a new pride that is more sinful
still.[2] Her son Gustave is as empty as his father; worse still, her
daughter Geneviève shares her contempt for Robert: 'I am afraid
of finding in her my own thoughts, but bolder, so bold that they
terrify me.' She has an explanation with Robert, and tells him that
because he is 'very different from the man I loved', she must leave
him. Robert weeps desperately and says, 'If you still loved me a
little, you would understand that I am only a poor, struggling
creature, like anyone else, who tries as best he can to be a little
better than he is.' He loves her still: then it is her duty to stay.
But war breaks out, and Robert contrives to get not only a safe
job, but the Croix de Guerre with it. This is the last straw, or rather,
perhaps, a longed-for sufficient excuse. Éveline leaves him to
become a nurse in a war hospital, where a dangerous disease is
treated – she does not say precisely which.

Gide's original theme, already complex enough, had become, as
always, further modified and involuted by irony. Only the un-

[1] Gide slyly alludes to the title of Pierre Louÿs' novel, *The Woman and the
Puppet*, where the words have a very different implication.

[2] For a more extended discussion of humility, humiliation, and pride see the
Second Lecture of Gide's *Dostoevsky*, in particular the words: 'If humility is a renunciation of pride, humiliation leads, on the contrary, to a reinforcement of
pride.'

wary reader will see Éveline as a cruelly wronged woman, or Robert as her mediocre inferior. In Éveline's early journal there is a triple meaning: behind her ecstatic admiration of Robert we infer his actual deficiencies; but she reveals herself as equally mediocre and much sillier. Her powers of analysis are keen, but directed exclusively to the faults of others; her sin is not so much pride as vanity. In her marriage she shows that inability of the twentieth-century matron to exist as an individual apart from her family, that tendency to avenge her discontent upon her husband, which Mr Lewis Way has so acutely exposed in his *Man's Quest for Significance*.

The critics, missing the point, raised an outcry against Gide's harsh treatment of Robert. Reverting to the method of Browning's *Ring and the Book*, he conceived the amusing idea of re-telling the story from Robert's point of view. He produced *Robert* in a single week in September 1929; it was a facility he often showed when, as with Alissa's journal in *Strait is the Gate*, he wrote from within the mind of an alien personality, instead of toiling to distinguish an avatar from himself.

In *Robert* (which its putative author says might be called *The School for Husbands*), Robert writes in angerless sorrow to Gide, remonstrating against his indiscretion in releasing to the public the private journal of another man's wife. Robert is equally devoid of resentment against Éveline. She had wounded, with her contempt, his heart, but not his vanity; indeed, paradoxically, Robert has less vanity, and more genuine self-respect, than Éveline. His remark in 1894, which Éveline first admired and later despised, was perfectly sincere, however complacent: 'I want success not for myself, but for the ideas I represent.' Éveline 'claimed the right to judge every-thing for herself'. Robert, submissive to an ideal external to him-self, mimics virtues he does not possess, as a means of coming to possess them. Éveline, with her friends, Dr Marchant and the painter Bourgweilsdorf, 'confused with hypocrisy, or at least insincerity, every striving towards perfection, every subordination of sensation and emotion to an ideal'. 'What Éveline despised in me, was that effort towards better things which was the only thing in me that was not despicable.' 'She refused to understand that I could prefer in myself the person I wanted to be, and tried to become, to the person I naturally was.' 'What cruel misunderstandings are caused in love,' he sighs, 'by not seeing the beloved for what he is, but making of him a sort of idol; and then holding it against him that he is something else, as if he could help it.' Robert concludes by revealing that he has married again, this time happily; and it is with his second wife that he awaits eternal union in the life to come. 'We are making for different heavens, my dear,' Éveline had once said.

Robert, a conservative, a Catholic, a servant of spiritual authority, is everything against which Gide had set his whole life. Yet, despite the rich comedy he draws from Robert's fatuity, he does him, as he had done the prodigal's elder brother, such justice as almost to let him win the case. Robert is an imbecile, but no villain; perhaps, although there could be no progress if all were like Robert, if none were like Robert no progress could be retained. Gide, too, had bowed to duty and constraint; and in 1938, in the despair that followed his wife's death, he recommended to himself, with only a little self-irony, 'Robert's method': to imitate a victory he has not yet reached, in order to attain it.

In March 1930, six months after *Robert* and in the middle of *Oedipus,* Gide began *Geneviève,* the narrative of Robert's daughter. At first he intended Geneviève to reach her salvation by the route he himself was following, that of communism; but on New Year's day, 1932, he suddenly saw the artistic mistake of making an imaginary character a literal vehicle for his own opinions, and the possibility of writing a great work on communism. The book on communism was never to be written; meanwhile, he successfully purged *Geneviève* of the communist ideas he meant to reserve for the other. In 1933 *Geneviève* as we have it was written, though twice, at Syracuse in February 1934 and in West Africa in March 1936, he began and destroyed a Part Three. Despairing of completing a novel that had never deeply interested or convinced him ('I owe it to my heroine to remain reasonable,' he complained), he published the fragment in 1939; and there the matter rests at present.

Geneviève, in turn, has sent Gide her version of the family history. Like her hated father, she views Gide's work with irony.

He has answered 'in a vague and general manner, the question: of what is man capable?' But the problem for her is: 'What, in our day, has a woman the power and right to hope?' Hitherto feminine virtue has been negative, consisting in devotion, submission, and fidelity – to man. Her mother could only long for freedom; for Geneviève it is a question of taking it – but how, and for what ends?

At school she falls in love with Sara, ravishing daughter of a Jewish painter, and one of the last of the bastards in Gide's novels. Sara is obsessed with the idea of freedom in love without the slavery of marriage, and succeeds in transmitting her views to Geneviève, before Éveline, detecting her daughter's peril, separates them. Geneviève reads *Jane Eyre* and *Clarissa*. 'Women need exercise for their faculties as much as their brothers do,' she found in the former; but of the latter she says: 'This equating of honour with chastity seemed to me inadmissible' – 'Dishonour consists not in having a lover, but in being kept by a man.' She takes up the study of law in order to ascertain the rights of women, and asks Dr Marchant to give her a child. He refuses, and she recognizes that her object was not love for him, still less desire for the child, but to defy convention, and in particular her father. She visits Éveline, who is to die a few months later, in her war hospital, and finds that her mother had been in love with Dr Marchant, and that here must have lain, in part, his motive for refusing the daughter.

In *Geneviève* Gide meant 'boldly to tackle the whole question of feminism'; there is no sign here or elsewhere that he felt it had a solution. Geneviève wishes to discover something that only women can do, to do it herself and help other women to do it. 'Feminine qualities can be different from masculine without being inferior.' She has the same motto as Bernard in *The Coiners*: '*You* can do it.' Do what? Presumably in Part Three she would have found out; or perhaps Gide could not complete Part Three because he, too, was unable to answer 'the whole question of feminism': what is it that only a woman can do? And perhaps the only answer is, 'to have a baby'; and this, at least, Geneviève was to do, for she mentions her son, and without marrying, for she is still a spinster. Can it be that the future father of her child would have been Bernard of *The Coiners*? Bernard, we know, was to appear in Part Three. But it would have been an unsatisfactory meeting: Geneviève is his feminine counterpart, and has discovered for herself his motto, but she is hardly his equal. And another of her sayings, 'It doesn't matter how we get there, if we know where we are going,' is the exact opposite of Bernard's 'It doesn't matter where we are going, provided we advance.'

Is the theme of Gide's trilogy wholly imaginary, or is it drawn from real life? Possibly when Gide's entire correspondence comes to be published, we may find traces, in his family or friends, of a menage resembling Robert and Éveline's. Certainly a few traits in Robert are taken from Eugène Rouart: his mingling of culture, politics, and business, his progressive conventionalization, and his way of saying, when he pretends that someone else's idea is his own, 'I looked for it, and I found it.'[1] There are elements in Éveline of Gide's friend and companion Mme Théo van Rysselberghe, in Geneviève of her daughter Élisabeth, the mother of Gide's daughter Catherine. But the point has less importance in this, the most impersonal of Gide's fictions, than elsewhere.

In 1930 Gide launched a documentary series of crime-dossiers under the title *Ne jugez pas* (*Judge Not*). It was a return to the preoccupation of his *Souvenirs de la cour d'assises* (*Memories of the Assize Court*) of 1914. From 13 to 25 May 1912, after insisting that his name should be included in the list of jurors, he had sat in the jury at the Rouen assizes, and 'felt to the point of anguish how dubious and precarious is human justice.' It is hardly correct to relate this experience, as some critics have, to his interest at that time in the 'gratuitous act'. The crimes of theft and rape, on which he had to pronounce guilty or not guilty, were the animal reactions of sub-normal people to the unhappiness of their environment; they are striking, indeed, in the absence of real profit or pleasure to the criminal, but they never approach the dignity of gratuity, nor does he ever mention that august theme in this

[1] Related of Rouart in the *Journal* for 19 August 1927.

connection. The interest here is social and moral rather than psychological. The evidence, he found, was recurrently obscure; he intervened several times, but found the points he raised were too subtle for judge or jury; the machine of justice ground on, 'creaking hideously.'

L'Affaire Redureau (The Redureau Case) presented, on the other hand, a genuine 'gratuitous act'. In 1913 Marcel Redureau, a boy of fifteen, being reprimanded by his employer, had killed him, his wife, their children, servants, the baby, everyone in the house – a total of seven persons. He could not explain why he did it, and was awarded twenty years' imprisonment.

In La Séquestrée de Poitiers (The Prisoner of Poitiers) the interest is even more exclusively psychological. In 1901 an anonymous letter revealed to the police of Poitiers that Mélanie Bastian had been incarcerated by her severe mother and malleable brother, ever since the birth of an illegitimate child in 1875. The unfortunate girl, now an emaciated half-wit of fifty-one, was removed to hospital, where she wept and begged to be taken back to her 'dear little grotto,' to the 'dear good big place' where she had lain contented in filth and nakedness for twenty-five years. The mother died in prison before trial, the brother was condemned and then acquitted on appeal. Evidence showed that he had been dominated by his mother; that in him, as in the rest of the family, there was a marked love of solitude and unpleasant odours; and that Mélanie had been lavishly fed on chicken, filleted sole and wine, in the debris of which round her bed rioted cockroaches and mealworms. Gide has little comment to make; possibly he realized that the hidden cause of these monstrous effects could only be found in the psychology of Freud, whom he had dismissed as 'an imbecile of genius'. He first mentions the Poitiers case in 1926; but it is likely that he had taken note of it, and kept the records in his files, at the time of its appearance in the newspapers in 1901. If so, it is significant that Gertrude in Pastoral Symphony was discovered by the pastor in a similar state of verminous filth and apparent idiocy; and that Mélanie Bastian's pet name, by which her brother used to call her in their youth, was – Gertrude.

After The Prisoner of Poitiers Gide abandoned the collection of crime stories. Evidently it would be impossible to go further in horror, and pointless, having gone so far, to serve up anything less horrible. Then again, such actualities, though the truth and lucidity with which they are presented are highly aesthetic and typically Gidian, are only the raw material of art. But the chief reason for his change of direction was that his imagination was hurrying on from the particular to the general, from isolated evil in the underworld of the individual to mass evil in the underworld of humanity. The Gidian pendulum was swinging from the Dostoevskian to the Marxian.

For the first five years after the Congo, however, the chief symptoms in Gide's *Journal* of his new moral crisis are not the references, numerous as they are, to social injustice, but those, far more numerous, to religion, to the struggle (for he now regarded these two faiths as opposite and opposed) between Christianity and Catholicism, between freedom and authority, joy and gloom. His sense of encroaching old age, the waning of the desires of the flesh, was also at work in his new altruism; both feelings were largely illusory, for youth and desire never failed to return; but, as he remarked, 'lost desires leave the way open for moralizing.' This old battle, revived by new conversions of his friends[1] and their new attempts to convert himself, is the manifest, though not the latent, subject of *Oedipus*.

Gide's play was begun in June 1929, completed in November 1930, and published in 1931. Like Sophocles before him, he closely followed the unalterable legend. Oedipus, King of Thebes, goaded by the blind prophet Tiresias, discovers that the man he has killed in self-defence was his father, and the woman he has married is his mother: he blinds himself in retribution, and goes into exile. But Gide, with astonishing ingenuity, weaves a web of parallels between the condition of Oedipus and his own. The struggle between Oedipus and Tiresias is Gide's own conflict with his Catholic friends and enemies. Like Jammes and Claudel long ago, Tiresias tries to persuade him that he is soul-sick; like Du Bos, that he is

---

[1] Notably Copeau and Charles Du Bos. Of the latter's tendentious and wounding *Dialogue with André Gide*, Mme Théo van Rysselberghe said, 'He is riding to salvation on your back.'

unhappy. And like the Prodigal Son Oedipus suffers a spiritual
defeat (but voluntary, and therefore half a victory), against which
Gide himself was well inoculated. Less apparently, but perhaps
more fundamentally, Oedipus, like so many of Gide's works, is a
tragi-comedy of the family; and who could be more intimately
appropriate to the theme than the very founder of the Oedipus
complex? Gide's characters, by an ironic anachronism, are well
acquainted with the doctrines of Freud. Eteocles – like father, like
son – has designs on his sister Ismene; but 'I repress them', he says
complacently. And when Polynices suggests, 'There are heaps of
things we think about without knowing it', Eteocles adds, 'That is
what our dreams are made of'. The sons of Oedipus represent the
embarrassing band of young disciples who in the '20s, twenty
years out of date, seized on the 'inquietude' that had been Gide's
watchword in the 1900s. Marcel Arland in 1924 had written on
Le Nouveau mal du siècle, Daniel-Rops in 1926 on Notre Inquiétude,
and Eteocles is writing a treatise called The New Mal du siècle, or
Our Inquietude. 'Of my example,' says Oedipus, 'they have taken
only what flatters them, authorizations and licence, letting pass
constraint, the difficult and the better.' And in the situation of
Oedipus, symbol of a malady that every man carries, active or
encysted, in his unconscious, there is an allegory of the early death
of Gide's father, of Gide's half-incestuous marriage, immediately
he had lost his mother, with his cousin her substitute.[1] 'I feel for her
a love that is at once filial and conjugal,' says Oedipus of Jocasta.
Lastly, Oedipus's self-blinding and exile, which, by equating him
with the blind Tiresias, seems his final defeat, in fact represents
Gide's communist mission. It is a punishment and a relinquishment of his past egoistic blindness to reality, and the acceptance of
a new discipline. 'A great destiny awaits me, the time of my quiet-
ude is past,' says Oedipus; and 'I am a nameless traveller, who
renounces his glory, his goods, and himself.'

Gide's next work, though it, too, is drawn from Greek myth-
ology, is a still plainer parable of the necessity of communism. In
July 1934 Copeau and Ida Rubinstein staged a choral ballet,

---

[1] And in Jocasta's distress when Oedipus insists on publicity for his crime, there
is an echo of Madeleine Gide's at the publication of Corydon and If It Die. . . .

Persephone, with verse libretto by Gide, choreography by Kurt Jooss, and music by Stravinsky. For six months of the year, in the Greek legend, Persephone dwells among the dead in Hades with her husband and ravisher Pluto, and leaves the earth to joyless winter; and for six months she returns as goddess of spring, bringing flowers and new joy, and, with her second husband Triptolemus, harvest. But Gide, once again, has distilled a new and personal allegory from the Greek myth.

> How can I laugh and sing and put off care,
> Knowing a hungry people waits in pain?
> You draw me, sorrowful people of the shades,
> And I go to you . . .

says Persephone. Gide himself had recently visited a coalmine: the prisoners in the underworld are the workers, the miners, the 'lower' classes, and Persephone, who sees their misery by gazing into a narcissus, Gide's flower, is Gide himself. It was partly through gazing into himself that he had seen the necessity of social revolution. And Persephone regains her longing for the life of earth by eating a pomegranate, the fruit of the earth whose savour Gide had hymned in his youth forty years before. Gide's verse is an accomplished and delicious mingling of diluted Racine and diluted Valéry, completely appropriate to the modernized Gluck of Stravinsky's setting.

In 1935 Gide published his only major work written under the spell of communism. A few pages of *Later Fruits of the Earth* had appeared as early as 1921;[1] now, as then, in imminent expectation of death, he meant his book to be a testament of his old age, of importance corresponding to the *Fruits* of his youth. The early *Fruits* told of a joy that comes from excluding, in oneself, the darker side of human existence. Gide had immediately, even then, turned to the knowledge in himself of these stern realities, the cause and subject of his old 'inquietude', and by now he was unable to ignore them in others. The *Later Fruits* reaffirm the doctrine of the old, enlarged by, battling with, and reconciled to the new themes of suffering, death, old age, religion, 'social

---

[1] In Gide's *Morceaux choisis.*

questions', duty, progress; and the drama of his book lies in the victories gained, one by one, by the gospel of joy over the sombre facts that might well, it seemed, have defeated it. And to achieve these conquests, the old gospel is modified by the concept of happiness no longer as freedom, but as a submission to duty, a heroism. 'The happiness of man is not in freedom, but in the acceptance of a duty,' Gide had written in his preface to the aviator Saint-Exupéry's *Night-Flight*; and long ago, in 1910, he had exclaimed, 'Barrès! Barrès! Why don't you understand that what we need is not mental comfort, but heroism?'

The front of battle is first drawn up by a new alignment of the forces of joy, keen as ever, but matured, even senescent. Much of this Book One was inspired, no doubt, by the renaissance of ecstasy, in the early 1920s, which Gide owed to friendship with Marc Allégret; it is interspersed with ethereal lyrics in the manner of Rimbaud's verse *Illuminations*. In Book Two the tragic opposition is announced by a corresponding series of prose 'Encounters': a sorrowful Negro down and out in Paris, an unappreciated breeder of tropical fish, a lunatic in an asylum, a drowned child, Marc Allégret's brother Jean-Paul dying of tuberculosis in a sanatorium.[1] 'Why this tale,' asks Nathanael, 'in a book which you dedicate to joy?' and Gide replies, 'Truly, I do not want a happiness that springs from others' misery.'

Happiness in the individual is now necessary not in its own right, but for the sake of others. 'He who does not know how to be happy himself can do nothing for the happiness of others.' 'My happiness is to augment that of others. In order to be happy I need the happiness of all.' And his joy, therefore, though undiminished, is transposed from the present, in which he feels it, to the time when others will share it. For the first time Gide pronounces the word 'future,' hitherto suspect, with lyricism. 'I lean over that abyss, the future, without vertigo.' 'Today's Utopia is to-morrow's reality.' His reason has now joined his heart, he affirms, on the slope of communism; and that slope (he alludes to the maxim Bernard accepts from Édouard in *The Coiners*) 'seems to lead upward.' It is the only occasion in the *Later Fruits* where he

[1] At Arcachon, where Gide visited him in 1930.

names communism; but henceforth he addresses Nathanael as 'comrade'.

He reaffirms his love for Christ as the Messiah of happiness: 'Christ's first word is to embrace sadness itself in joy: "Blessed are those who weep." And he has little understanding of this word who sees in it nothing but an encouragement to weep!' 'It is you, Lord Christ,' he cries, 'that I find everywhere, when I believed that I was avoiding you, divine friend of my youth.' His belief in God reaches its nadir in the *Later Fruits*, yet, however ambiguously, survives. He holds a dialogue with God, in which the witty Almighty appallingly resembles the Millionaire of *Prometheus*; yet even now God, 'that confused mass of notions, sentiments, appeals, and answers to those appeals, which I now know existed only through and in me', seems 'much more worthy of interest than the rest of the world and myself and the whole of humanity'. But religion is now the enemy not only of truth and freedom, but of progress; Gide's meaningful last word is: 'Do not sacrifice to idols.' Soon he was indignantly to withdraw his own sacrifice from a different idol, which he had temporarily mistaken for a true god.

At a period in the early 1920s when Gide's conversion to Catholicism again seemed imminent, a Catholic friend had remarked: 'I hope it won't happen too soon, because it wouldn't last long' – and so it was to be with Gide's communism, his only conversion,[1] and therefore his only false step. The false step, however, was a misunderstanding, not an inconsistency. Gide did not come to believe, and then cease to believe, in a principle; he became convinced on hearsay that the principle in which he already believed was incarnate in Soviet Russia. He was converted not so much to communism, as to a delusion that communists were already Gidians.

For the only time in his life Gide was guilty of believing what he wished to believe; yet the causes of his surrender go far to excuse him. He had always maintained that the Kingdom of Heaven must be set up on earth, not postponed to the far side of the grave.

[1] The word 'conversion' is convenient, but not wholly fair; Gide himself rejected it, and wrote only of 'adhesion', 'rallying', 'decision'.

His friends among the French communists, Dabit, Jef Last, Pierre
Herbart, Malraux, were intelligent, sincere, and men of good
will – how could he foresee that in sharing their aims, he was
sharing their deception? And in those days the Soviet Union was
wooing Western intellectuals by telling them only what they
wished to hear. Stalin's denunciations of capitalism, Gide knew,
were thoroughly justified; and the connoisseur in the wiles of
the devil allowed himself to forget that it is often Satan who best
rebukes sin.

Both in his *Journal* and in his rare public utterances he made clear
the special nature of the communism to which he 'adhered'. 'I feel
a brother only to those who have come to communism through
love,' he wrote; and again, 'what leads me to communism is not
Marx but the Gospels'; and he quoted with approval Marx's
epigrammatic 'I am not a Marxist.' Even so soon, he felt misgivings: 'Conversion to communism, like that to Catholicism,
implies submission to a dogma, recognition of an orthodoxy – and
to me all orthodoxies are suspect.' And in 1934 he sent a message
to the Congress of Soviet Writers in Russia, in which he affirmed
that in the realm of the intellect the task of the USSR was to
inaugurate a 'communist individualism' in art and literature. But
the most revealing document outside the *Journal* is the account
(published as *André Gide et Notre Temps*) of a public debate,
held in January 1935, between Gide, Massis, Mauriac, Maritain,
and others. 'I wish to believe,' he confessed, 'that an alliance
between art and communist doctrine is possible, but I have
been unable to find the point of fusion. That is why I have
produced nothing for four years;[1] and undoubtedly this is a
sacrifice.' Massis expressed himself with perfect decency – so did
Gide – and the occasion passed off without unpleasantness; indeed,
the most remarkable feature of the debate was the genuine concern
shown by Gide's opponents, at seeing their beloved enemy following so dangerous a path. The feeling was shared by his colleagues
of the *NRF*. 'Your thought is disposed to affirmations that are
pure acts of faith,' wrote Jean Schlumberger in a leading article,
'you ought first to go there and see.' And in June 1936, shortly after

[1] He published nothing between *Oedipus* in 1931 and *Later Fruits* in 1935.

a brief trip to West Africa, Gide took up the challenge, and visited Russia, with Dabit, Jef Last, Herbart and others, as guest of the Soviet Government.

In Russia he hoped to see nothing less than a country where everyone was happy. This eternal traveller had never set out for a land more fabulous; but before, he had never been disappointed. It is a question how far the shock of his disappointment has distorted his account of Russia in *Back from the USSR*. He relates facts – but the reader is likely to be swayed rather by the flavour of bitterness, of hope betrayed, with which Gide sets them down. Some of his complaints are surely unfair: he had foreseen and refuted many of them – they are, in fact, the usual ones – in a *Journal* entry for 30 January 1932. Industrial inefficiency, onanism and an unsolved housing problem are not peculiar to Russia; and few but Gide – or Ménalque – would reproach the Soviet with failure to destroy the family. It is curious, too, that on his arrival every face he saw was beaming with energy and joy, while later, when his faith was destroyed, everyone seemed oppressed, stupid, despairing. But the overall insight of his indictment is such, that it needed the cold war of post-war Stalinism to reveal its full profundity and surprise one with its topicality. Again and again, as when he notes the Soviet's persuading the people that everyone is less happy in other countries, and to that end preventing communication with the outside world; the replacement of the old spirit of revolution with a new spirit of conformism; the forcing of composers and writers to follow the party line – 1936 in the clear sight of Gide resembles the 1950s and 1960s.

In *Back from the USSR* and *Afterthoughts on the USSR* Gide hastened to announce his mistake. It is, perhaps, the necessary speed of their composition, as much as their factual and political nature, and their angry bitterness, that makes these, alone of his works, artistically unsatisfying. They are the final payment in the long sacrifice of his art to 'social preoccupations' – 'since these began to encumber my head and heart, I have written nothing of value.'[1] 'If I was mistaken, it is best to recognize my error as soon as may be; for I am responsible, here, to those whom this error

[1] *Journal*, 5 September 1936.

leads astray.' And he obeyed his duty to the greater cause of truth; for 'it is to the truth that I attach myself, and if the Party leaves the truth, then I leave the Party.'[1] But, always, it was not the revolution, but the betrayal of the revolution that he condemned. 'The errors peculiar to one country do not suffice to compromise the truth of a cause that is international and universal.' Now, however, that the true revolution must be awaited elsewhere than from Russia, he sought it again in the Gospels that had led him to communism. 'The break-down of communism restores to Christianity its revolutionary implications.' Looking back, in the *Journal* for 7 February 1940, he wrote: 'Slowly I came to convince myself, that when I thought myself a communist, I was in fact a Christian.'

After the publication of his book, *Pravda* paid him an involuntary compliment: 'Gide is the typical representative of a decadent bourgeoisie; he is an individualist.' And when in August 1937 Gide visited Italy and found everywhere the slogan 'Believe, obey, fight', chalked on the walls, he remarked that the words would suit Moscow as well as Italy.

[1] Not literally, for Gide had never become a party-member.

THE END OF MARRIAGE

Et Nunc Manet in Te

'Yesterday evening I thought of her; I talked to her, as I often did, more easily in imagination than in her real presence; when suddenly I said to myself: But she is dead.' – *Et Nunc Manet in Te*.

Between the entries for April and August of 1938 a thick black line is ruled across the page of Gide's *Journal*. This symbol of mourning and catastrophe marks the death of Mme Gide on 17 April; and the months in which he records his 'disorder, distress and despair', 'in order that some other, desperate as I, may feel himself less alone when he reads me', are the most nobly moving of all Gide's sixty years of diaries. He spent the summer at Cuverville, the Prodigal's House, where she had always remained, and to which he had always returned. 'Since she is here no longer,' he cries, 'invitations to happiness are a vexation.' His freedom is that of 'a kite when the string that constrained it is cut'; he has fallen to earth. But when she was alive, he never allowed her love to falsify his thought; 'and now she is gone, I must not allow my thought to be crushed by the memory of that love'. 'If I cannot reach serenity again, my philosophy is bankrupt.'

It is no easy matter to be the wife of a great writer; it is no easier for a great writer to endure marriage. General opinion (usually, whether for or against homosexuality, with an obvious axe to grind) has drawn from *The Immoralist* and *Corydon*, even from the remorseful and self-condemnatory *Et Nunc Manet in Te*, a distorted view of Gide's marriage. The real and sufficient evidence, despite the well-known entry of February 1912[1], is in the *Journal*; and it

[1] 'One of the best conversations I have ever had with Em. – but of everything that relates to her I forbid myself to speak here.'

must now be examined, with proper reverence but in good faith, both as an answer to calumny and for its intrinsic importance in Gide's life and work. When both the constant factors and the evolution of his married life have been discovered, we can proceed, as he did himself, to estimate its general significance.[1]

The epoch of the 1890s has already been discussed; with the conclusion that, while a real conflict between freedom and duty lies behind *The Immoralist*, Gide was a less cruel husband than Michel, and Mme Gide a less ill-used wife than Marceline.[2] Husband and wife travelled for the most part together, until prevented by Mme Gide's ill-health: this was their honeymoon period. Between 1898 and 1900, the time of his prowlings on the boulevard and the mysterious relinquishment of La Roque, Gide reclaimed his sexual freedom, and gradually compromised on his freedom to travel. Tunisia was abandoned in 1903, but replaced by recurrent visits to Italy, of which the *Journal* mentions seven between 1908 and 1914; on two of them Gide notes that he wrote to his wife every day. This was the period of the supremacy of Cuverville, the House to which the Prodigal returned; of his life there Gide wrote in May 1906: 'Her affection, her charm, her poetry make round her a kind of radiance in which I warm myself, and in which my sadness melts.' When the longing for travel carried him away, it was mingled with regret: 'Em. can never know how my heart is torn at the thought of leaving her, and in order to find happiness far from her'; 'going was not enough for me: I needed also Em.'s approval of my going.'[3] During the first half of the war they were drawn together by the common anxiety, the impossibility of travel, and their works of charity, hers at Cuverville, his in Paris; in 1917

---

[1] Many of the crucial entries will be quoted below; but those who desire amplification should spend a pleasant hour looking up the references to Mme Gide in the admirable index to Mr Justin O'Brien's translation of the *Journal*. Much new evidence appeared after Gide's death in *Et Nunc Manet in Te*, with its hitherto suppressed entries from his *Journal*, and in Jean Schlumberger's *Madeleine et André Gide* (a sincere book, equitable in intention, though a little biassed in favour of the wife and against the husband) with its extracts from Mme Gide's letters.

[2] And less spineless – we have the formidable figure of Alissa to set off against Marceline.

[3] *Journal*, November 1904.

Gide finds with approval that the item 'Gifts' has made up a quarter of the year's expenditure. From their marriage until this time they continued to visit theatres and museums together, and Gide retained his childhood pleasure in reading aloud to his cousin, with the object of seeing aesthetic experience through her mind as well as his own: there could be no more striking proof of the persistence, however relative, of the spiritual intimacy of their childhood. For some years, however, the radiance of their marriage was to be overclouded, though not finally extinguished.

In 1916 came the crisis, soon to be followed by worse, which together with Mme Gide's discovery of Ghéon's incriminating letter formed the hidden personal drama of *Numquid et tu . . .?* Gide hoped to spend the winter with his new love Élisabeth van Rysselberghe, who later suggested in part both Gertrude in *Pastoral Symphony* and Laura in *The Coiners*; but 'I think only of giving up this plan, like so many others, since I should have to buy my happiness at the cost of hers,' he wrote,[1] and did not go. His next plan, however, he did not abandon, but bought at this cost. From 1917 onwards Marc Allégret became the object of numerous escapes from Cuverville. On 21 November 1918, soon after returning to Cuverville from his four months in England with Marc, Gide learned of the terrible destruction of his letters, by which his wife symbolized her disbelief not only in his present love for her but in the pure love of their youth. In January 1923 she was distressed by 'what seems to her a lamentable catastrophe', the birth of Élisabeth van Rysselberghe's daughter Catherine. 'I have always thought it a bad thing that Élisabeth was brought up without religion,' she sternly commented. Did she know the identity of the 'father unknown' under whom this birth was registered? 'I have never known whether my wife had suspicions or a certainty,' Gide told Claude Mauriac many years later. But a perhaps unformulated instinct had told her even of the child's conception in the previous July, when Gide was at Hyères with Élisabeth van Rysselberghe. So it seemed to Gide himself, when on 7 August he received a letter from her: she had given to her god-daughter Sabine Schlumberger the gold necklace and little emerald

[1] *Journal*, 7 October, 1916.

cross that she had worn in girlhood, like Alissa in *Strait is the Gate*.
By a heartrending irony she had told him in 1894, when still
adamant in her refusal to marry him: 'If André has a daughter and
I am her godmother, I shall give her my little cross.' And when
Catherine was born, she need but count the months, although these
were only seven.

Their estrangement in the next few years was a weary and
hopeless truce, rather than a further worsening in their relationship;
it was also one-sided. 'She acts towards me constantly as though I
had ceased to love her; and I act towards her as though she loved
me still,' he wrote – and again: 'I have not ceased to love her, even
at the time when I seemed to be, and she had the right to think me,
farthest from her – to love her more than myself, more than life;
but I could no longer tell her so.' The manifestations of her distress
became, perhaps unconsciously, the instruments of her passive
revenge. She destroyed her beauty, neglected her health, abandoned
her music and reading (especially her husband's works) for house-
wifery and pious tracts. When he was committed to his conflict
with the Catholicism that had taken his friends she became, by
lingering degrees, a Catholic, though without formally joining
the Church. In their atrocious struggle, on his side to force her to
accept his devotion, on hers to disprove its existence, they each
inflicted and underwent the most appalling suffering; for if the
behaviour of each is measured by its effect upon the victim, Mme
Gide in her anguish gave almost as good as she got.

'The approval of a single simple decent man – that is the one
thing that matters to me, and that your book will not get,' she
said, expressing her hostility to the works (*Corydon, If It Die . . .*
and *The Coiners*) in which Gide gave his most important message
and, to her mind, too openly revealed himself. 'I tremble for you
because you are vulnerable, and you know it, and I know it,' she
told him;[1] meaning, by these terrible words, that he had not only
exposed himself to his enemies, but that their attacks would be
justified. 'Vulnerable . . .' Gide comments, 'I was so only through
her, and since then, it is all the same to me, and I fear nothing any
more. What have I to lose that I still care for?' 'The game is lost,

[1] *Journal,* 3 January 1922.

which I could win only with her,' he writes on 12 May 1927; and he compares her to Creusa, Eurydice, and Ariadne, the wives who lagged behind in order to force their husbands to look back. The estrangement, however, should not be exaggerated. It is marked chiefly by the disappearance of Mme Gide from the *Journal* from 1924 to 1928; it did not amount to separation, for throughout the period Gide's visits to Cuverville were undiminished.

In a little journal, her first since girlhood, which Madeleine Gide kept during his journey to the Congo in 1925–6, a return to tenderness is seen, as she imagines his travels, prays for his safety, and longs for his homecoming. At this time she was a match even for the formidable Claudel, who, vainly glimpsing a last opportunity of converting his beloved enemy, invited her to discuss with him 'a soul that is dear to you, and to which God has placed the key in your hands'. 'All who love André Gide as that very noble soul deserves to be loved,' she replied with magnificent loyalty, 'have the duty of praying for him. I do so every day – you also, do you not? – It is in this way, I believe, that you and I best meet in our desire for his best good.' For their wedding anniversary in 1928 she wrote: 'I think that later, when all things are revealed to us, we shall know that the 8th October was not a mistake, as I thought ten years ago, in the pain and bitterness of those days.'

And suddenly, in 1929, a reconciliation is evident. Gide and his wife visit their museums again, and readings aloud continue until shortly before her death. During the 1930s he began repeatedly to take stock of what he had gained by her constraint. 'My thought made up in depth what it lost in impetus';[1] 'without Em., who orientated my pious inclinations, I should not have written *André Walter,* or *The Immoralist,* or *Strait is the Gate,* or *Pastoral Symphony* etc. – or even, perhaps, *The Vatican Swindle* and *The Coiners* as a revolt and protest.'[2] Similarly, in the *Journal* of 9 June 1928 he had written, 'it was for him (Marc Allégret), to win his attention and his esteem, that I wrote *The Coiners,* just as I had written all my preceding books under the influence of Em., or in the vain hope of

[1] *Journal,* 29 June 1930.
[2] *Journal,* 16 June 1931.

convincing her'. And in the *Journal* of 6 January 1933: 'Every time I see her again, I realize that I have never really loved anyone but her – even, at times, it seems that I love her more than ever.' After fifty years, the 'mystic orientation of his life', which he discovered in his cousin's room at Rouen, still pointed in him unimpaired.

Mme Gide was important not so much because she brought Gide anything new, as in helping him not to lose what he already possessed. Before his marriage, at the time of *André Walter*, he already had in abundance the piety, the sense of the value of duty, constraint and sacrifice, that were characteristic of his cousin. At the time of his Tunisian liberation, and on other occasions later, he was in danger of losing all these: he married, and his wife's influence, perpetuating in assimilable form that of his dead mother, made possible the 'Gidian oscillation', and incalculably enriched his work and life. Without this centripetal force he might have degenerated, in the bonds of absolute freedom, into a Ménalque, a Wilde. She had changed his parabola into an orbit. His cousin Paul Gide had been amazed when Gide had wanted to take Mme Gide with him when he climbed mountains; and Gide had replied: 'What matters to me is not going far myself, but rather taking someone else with me.' If she had not consented to go with him, or at least to wait for his return, he would either have gone too far or never have travelled. In the beginning, long ago in the 1880s, two children had read together in the lamplight until each became the other in a rare and indestructible union of soul. They chose their marriage, and enacted its deep anguish and still deeper harmony to the full. Neither in the end would have wished not to have fulfilled this destiny.

In the autumn of 1938, a few months after his wife's death, Gide began to tell the secret history of their marriage in *Et Nunc Manet in Te*, which he completed in February 1939 at Luxor in Egypt, characteristically alternating his task by idyllic amours with little Ali and the garden-boys of his hotel, and by describing these in his *Carnets d'Égypte*. As he had done with *Corydon*, he protected his book against possible mishaps, such as a change of mind in his lifetime or posthumous expurgation, by privately printing thirteen copies in 1947 for distribution to friends; and a public edition appeared, as he had arranged, shortly after his own death in 1951. The title – 'and now she survives in thee' – was taken from a minor poem of Virgil, the *Culex*, and signifies the consolatory and true feeling that the lost beloved lives on undying in the heart and memory of the bereaved, rather than (as an indignant friend supposed) the 'narrowly egocentric point of view' that death had now annihilated Madeleine Gide for everyone except himself. On the contrary Gide ensured, with all or more than all due self-inculpation and remorse, that the real presence of his wife, with all her virtues and sorrows, should not be lost in the grave. As so often, his title has a double meaning, and the message 'and now she survives in thee' is addressed also to the understanding reader of his book.

It is only for the Pharisee that *Et Nunc Manet in Te* seems a merely shocking or discouraging book. This is not the story of a crime, nor even of two crimes, but the story, heroic and exemplary, of a tragedy. Gide and his wife, like every other married couple (as T. S. Eliot seems to say in *The Cocktail Party*), were trapped in a permanent dilemma, and through each other knew the human situation, with its nobility and despair, more profoundly than is possible in any other relationship. Given their special exigences and destiny, it was impossible for either of them to act more virtuously than they did; and their struggle for virtue was arduous and genuine, as was their love, as was their suffering. *Et Nunc Manet in Te* is a document of extreme and perpetual interest in the casebook of human morality. It is perhaps the most painful, certainly not the least beautiful and moving, of Gide's works.

SERENITY

The Journal, Imaginary Interviews, Theseus, So Be It

'The only art that pleases me is that which sets out from unrest and makes for serenity.' – *Journal*, 23 November 1940.

In 1939, the seventieth year of his life, Gide published the first fifty years of his *Journal*. Some regard it as his greatest work. It is in fact, as he says himself, a receptacle for everything he thought not quite worth putting into a work of art. But the contents of a great writer's wastepaper basket can add up to a whole not incommensurate with the sum of his deliberate creations. The integrity of his uniquely harmonious life as an artist, of his half-century of uninterrupted power and production, gives his *Journal* the unity of a work of art. In it his prose style, elsewhere more consciously finished, is unsurpassed in speed, limpidity, incisiveness and wit. The *Journal* makes the reader feel more intelligent, observant, sensual, charitable, free: and as an opportunity for day-to-day association with genius in process of thought and creation it stands, otherwise alone, with Keats's *Letters* and Flaubert's *Correspondance*.

'Free as never before, terribly free, shall I be able once more *to try to live?*' he wrote in the last sentence of his collected *Journal*.[1] In the spring of 1939 he made a journey in Egypt and Greece, strangely parallel to his Turkish march of 1914; but then he had looked in vain for a past bliss, and now he had his future *Theseus* in mind. The war duly came: 'Yes,' he wrote, 'this effort of culture that seemed to us so admirable (and I don't mean the French one

[1] The reference is to the last verse of Valéry's *Cimetiére marin* – 'The wind is up, and we must try to live.'

only) might well disappear – a bomb can get the better of a museum.' And yet, 'it is by championing the value of the particular, by her force of individualization, that France can and must best oppose the enforced unification of Hitlerism'.

During the war the seventy-year-old Gide conducted a one-man 'resistance' of his own – it was, so to speak, a passive resistance, but as heroic in its way as that of the young existentialists. His love of country fortified his independence of spirit: 'The more I feel myself a Frenchman,' he wrote, after refusing an invitation to broadcast and join in 'the emission of oxygen', 'the more I shun letting my thought be influenced – "enlistment" would destroy all its value.' He even welcomed Pétain's seemingly noble first speech after the capitulation: the words 'since the victory of 1918 the spirit of pleasure has won the day over the spirit of sacrifice' might have been spoken by this latter-day Gide himself. A few days later he heard, 'with stupor', Pétain denounce the Free French and England. 'This dishonour is the cruellest of our defeats,' he cried. Yet defeat and the Occupation were temporarily facts – 'what is the use of wounding ourselves by beating against the bars of our cage?' – 'the greatest danger for thought is to let itself be dominated by hatred.' By 'an acceptation which does not involve the inner being', 'the flower of civilization must be maintained.' 'I remember that in 1914,' he wrote, 'if they had listened to me, there would have been nothing but vegetables in the garden at Cuverville. How much wiser was my wife, who would not allow me to suppress the flowers!'

For two years Gide remained, an 'interior *emigré*', in the south of France, at Cabris with his daughter, at Nice or Vence with the family of Mme Dorothy Bussy, his incomparable translator and friend. His old enemies, including Béraud, collaborated industriously. Drieu La Rochelle, a sincere fascist who deserved his death by suicide in 1945 perhaps less than others who escaped the firing-squad, gained possession of the N R F. He invited Gide to make act of presence in Paris, and Gide replied by telegram: 'Appreciate your cordial letter, regret duty to request removal of my name from the wrapper of your review.'

During 1941 and 1942 Gide published in *Le Figaro* a series of

Imaginary Interviews which, among his works since *Journey to the Congo*, were excelled only by *Later Fruits* and *Theseus*. He had regained the humour and gaiety and permanent topicality of *Marshlands*, radiant now with an old man's serene courage and optimism. The *Interviews* are, ostensibly, on the purest of literary themes, on grammar, prosody, rhyme, the future of poetry, and the novel. In fact, cutting the most mockingly habile arabesques on the thinnest of political ice, they sustain a brilliantly ramified and prolonged *double entendre* on the opposition between the French spirit and the banal infamy of Pétainism. Nevertheless, when their historical background has become apparently obsolete, the *Interviews* still retain their full significance; for the values they postulate are eternal and, by yet a third level of his meaning, Gide presents them as such. His principles have not changed in his old age, though their applications are inexhaustibly new. 'The dominant feature of my life,' he had said long before,[1] 'is not inconstancy, but fidelity.' 'At my age,' he mordantly tells the interviewer, 'we must be resigned to repeating ourselves, if we are not to talk nonsense.' The interest of Gide's later thought lies not in a continual changing of boats, but in the success with which his old ark rides new waves. As for the interviewer, he is, though something of a Pétainist and a Philistine, neither unintelligent nor unamiable. Gide treats him with irony but with good humour, and sends, through him, his message to all the young: 'Cease, I beg you, to believe there are gulfs between us. If you advance farther than we could, so much the better! – but it is, be sure, on the same road; where my good wishes and hopes will follow you, if they have not already gone before.' The interviewer, in his most favourable aspect, is the last of Gide's Nathanaels.

Gradually Gide had recovered from the crushing weight of despondency and 'acceptance', and regained energy for an intellectual action that was impossible even in 'unoccupied' France, and a solitude from which the affection of his friends had shielded him. In May 1942 he sailed for North Africa, and in December, during

[1] In the preface to the 1927 edition of *Fruits of the Earth*; where he continues: 'Name to me those who, before they die, can see that accomplished which they set out to accomplish – and I take my place beside them.'

the horror of the Allied air-raids on German-occupied Tunis, he was able to write: 'Ecstasy has become my normal state.' After the liberation of North Africa, when freedom seemed at last to ride the deluge, he launched an Algerian successor to the foundered *N R F* and called it *L'Arche* (*The Ark*). Then, in the clear air and white light of the city in which destiny had now united his fervent youth and serene old age, he called to mind the radiance of a yet more emblematic town, and wrote the tale of Theseus, builder of Athens.

The theme of *Theseus* had dwelt in Gide's imagination for fifty years. It is already implicit in a sentence of *Fruits of the Earth*: 'The memory of the past had only such power over me as was needed to give unity to my life; it was like the mysterious thread that held Theseus to his past love, yet did not prevent him from travelling through the newest of landscapes.' He echoes the thought in the *Journal* of 28 February 1912: 'Theseus risked himself amidst the labyrinth, assured by the secret thread of an inner fidelity.' But marriage had given an additional significance to Ariadne's thread: 'Ariadne, after he has slain the Minotaur, makes Theseus return to the point from which he set out,' he wrote, in the 'detached leaves' that follow the *Journal* of 1911[1] – and it is here that he first mentioned his intended book, for he proceeds: 'In the *Theseus* this must be brought out – to put it vulgarly, the thread is the apron-string.' On 18 January 1931 he imagines a meeting in old age between Oedipus and Theseus, 'each measuring himself by the other'; and on 16 September 1931 the subject of Dedalus and Icarus is added.

Gide's Theseus, like his Oedipus, keeps closely to the path traced for him by the stabilized and immemorial legend. He finds weapons by moving a rock, kills bandits, goes to Crete, overcomes the Minotaur in the labyrinth, abandons Ariadne and marries her sister Phædra, who falls in love with his son Hippolytus; and, having founded the city of Athens, he meets in old age the blinded

---

[1] Very likely written much earlier, for the same batch includes a note for the *Prodigal Son*, which must be dated before February 1907. The tale of Crete also appears in the epilogue to *Prometheus Misbound*. See also *Journal* for 12 May 1927 and 9 September 1940.

Oedipus. It is all extant, written in choice Greek by Euripides and Plutarch, and in still choicer French by Racine: all three of whom Gide consulted, but chiefly Plutarch. 'Have I not read this morning in Plutarch,' he had written in *Later Fruits*, 'at the beginning of the lives of Romulus and Theseus, that these two great founders of cities, from being born "secretly and of a clandestine union", were thought sons of gods?' Theseus is the last of Gide's bastard heroes.[1]

Once more, the thematic tension of Gide's work lies in the extraction, to fit his own preoccupations in particular, and those of mankind in general, of the symbolism already latent in the myth. The tales of Oedipus and Theseus come from a stratum of Greek legend which, preceding the civilized and adult era of the Trojan War, exploits the deepest childhood longings of individual and race. Oedipus kills his father and marries his mother – has it been noticed that Theseus does much the same, but in such a disguised form that he is able to survive, free from remorse, as a successful man of action? – whereas Oedipus is forced by an angry super-ego to punish himself by tearing out his eyes, a symbolic self-castration. Theseus cannot overtly marry his mother – but by a well-known mechanism of projection, the legend makes his wife Phædra pursue his guiltless son Hippolytus with a passion lethal to both. He cannot kill his father – but on his return from Crete he 'accidentally' drives the old man to suicide, by 'forgetting' to hoist the white sail. Gide's Theseus, well acquainted with the psychopathology of everyday life, is aware of the disguised wish implicit in his 'faulty act'. 'One can't think of everything,' he excuses himself, but adds, 'yet, if I analyse myself, which I never like doing, I can't swear it was really due to forgetfulness – Ægeus was in my way.' And he takes his father's place as King of Athens. Many an adult has been troubled by obscure guilt when his unconscious, still hiding a childhood wish and an infantile faith in its own omnipotence, has assumed responsibility for a father's natural death; and Gide, when his own father died, was only a boy of ten.

---

[1] The parentage of Oedipus was similarly obscure. The fantasy that they were begotten by an unknown and more distinguished father is common among those blessed or cursed with the Oedipus complex.

The feeling is not incompatible with affection: Gide had been fond of his father, and Theseus says, 'Ægeus, my father, was one of the best.'

In the minor characters of Theseus we may glimpse passing hints of persons of importance in Gide's past: in Hippolytus, whose loss 'was the great sorrow of my life', of Marc Allégret, Gide's adopted son; in Pirithous, the friend of his youth who grows intellectually opposed to him, of Marcel Drouin; in Dedalus, architect of the labyrinth, of Valéry; in Icarus, the sun-soaring and singed drug-addict, of Cocteau. As in *The Return* and *Strait is the Gate*, and very possibly in real life, the Gidian hero is loved by two sisters.[1] But Theseus, alone of the heroes Gide modelled on himself, is good, great, and successful, a hero indeed. Michel, Jerome, Lafcadio, the Pastor, Édouard, had been in their various ways misguided and ineffectual, wanderers in a labyrinth; they were self-purgings, rejected selves. Here, at last, in his Indian summer, Gide boldly asserts his claim as 'one who has seen accomplished that which he set out to accomplish'. 'I am content,' says the aged Theseus.

> I have fulfilled my destiny. Behind me I leave the town of Athens. I have cherished it even above my wife and son. I have built my city. After me my thought will be able to inhabit it eternally. It is without regret that I draw near my solitary death. I have tasted of the fruits of the earth. I am glad to think that after me, thanks to me, men will recognize themselves as happier, better, and more free. For the good of humanity to come I have accomplished my work. I have lived.

For eight years after *Theseus*, Gide's 'solitary death' receded before him. He continued to travel, with an old man's preference (which Housman shared before him) for the time-saving aeroplane; to bask in the sun of Nice, and the electric light of his library-study in Paris. In 1947 he received an honorary degree at Oxford (it required all the ardent energy of Miss Enid Starkie to induce

---

[1] And, as in *Strait is the Gate*, by their mother also. Pasiphaë, when she inserts her hand in the bosom of Theseus, employs the same method of seduction as Alissa's mother with Jerome and, it may be suspected, Madeleine Gide's adulterous mother with the boy André Gide.

that ancient university to honour itself by honouring him), followed in November by the Nobel Prize for Literature.

After the final manifesto and testament of *Theseus*, there was no room left for a new major work: he had 'fulfilled his destiny'. But the books of his last years show the unabated power and harmony of his fundamentally healthy genius. In 1946 appeared his *Journal* for 1939–42. In 1948 he published a prose translation of Shakespeare's *Hamlet*, which was produced with enormous success by his friend Jean-Louis Barrault, and a stage version of Kafka's *The Trial*. In 1949 came a volume of prefaces and essays called *Feuillets d'automne* (*Autumn Leaflets*) (a title typically punning on Hugo's *Feuilles d'automne*), and an *Anthology of French Poetry*, with a long and remarkable introduction on the nature of poetry. This volume should be read not only as the most important of all French anthologies, not only for its revelations of Gide's consummate personal taste; the reader should note the sly delight with which he has chosen anticipations, often involuntary, often in the most surprising quarters, of his own doctrines. He permitted the editing by others of his correspondence with Jammes and Claudel, and of *Littérature engagée*, a compilation of his speeches and articles in the time of his hitch-hike with communism, complete with a five-act 'comedy of characters', *Robert, or The Common Weal*, on which he had laboured in vain from 1934 to 1940. Fortunately this tiresome piece of left-wing propaganda is, as he himself reluctantly admitted,[1] Gide's only inferior work; devoid of his genius, crammed with lifeless good intentions, it may be excused as the exception that proves the rule. 'It took me almost as long to fail with *The Common Weal* as to succeed with *The Coiners*,' he wrote in 1949, 'Everything I wrote at that time, *invita Minerva*, remained unspeakably mediocre.'

Claudel, for the last quarter of a century, had remained implacable. 'That,' he gleefully exclaimed one day at lunch, at the sight of a pancake cooking in flaming brandy, 'is how Gide's soul will burn in hell!' Gide particularly enjoyed this anecdote of the

---

[1] 'My best friends unite in agreeing that it is very bad,' he wrote in the preface, 'I know that if I had always listened to them I should have published hardly anything... but I rather fear that as far as this play is concerned, my friends are right.'

crêpe flambée, still more when a son of Francis Jammes and godson of Claudel confided to him: 'Now I know that I'm not on their side, but on yours.' One of Claudel's numerous grandsons brought for signature the volume of the Gide–Claudel correspondence, already signed by grand-papa with the words: 'With my regret for being found in such bad company'; and Gide gravely wrote in it: 'Ditto'. 'Experts have assured me,' he remarked to Jean Lambert, the husband of his daughter Catherine, 'that I am a better Christian than Claudel.'

The more Christianly chivalrous Mauriac maintained that 'nothing need make us despair of the salvation of our friend'. But the views of Claudel, the self-appointed Grand Inquisitor of France, were to be upheld after Gide's death when, on 24 May 1952, '*Opera omnia Andreae Gide*' were placed by the Church on the *Index Librorum Prohibitorum*. Even so, the leader-writer in *Osservatore Romano,* the official journal of the Vatican, spoke worthily on this occasion of 'that strong sweet voice which recalls at times the loftiest utterance of all that is great in France'. In *Numquid et tu . . . ?* and elsewhere Gide had done his utmost to show the Church that the gulf between Her teachings and those of the Gospels is not as unbridgeable as it seems. Those works, to read which is now a mortal sin, are in one of their most important aspects a description unparalleled in modern times of the search for God, which Pascal assures us is one of the means of possessing Him: 'thou wouldest not seek Me, if thou hadst not already found Me.' It is permissible to see both the Catholic insistence on possession and the Protestant insistence on the search, and the eternal civil warfare of these principles, as indispensable parts of man's religious experience.

Lastly, in 1950, Gide published a final volume of the *Journal,* written during the years 1942–9. Gide's *Journal* covers a period of sixty years; in the last two decades the old man's daily thought, the quality he calls his 'inner azure', is keen and youthful as ever. His moments of fatigue and dejection are no more frequent and no less temporary than before, and he was never more alert, harmonious, and joyful. But the tone of the light has shifted, and the appreciation of this nuance is one of the special pleasures of sharing in his life's last quarter. In the '90s the radiance of the *Journal* was like a first fine day in spring; in the '30s and '40s it is a first cool day in autumn. 'Fervour' and 'liberation' had been the watchwords of his youth, 'inquietude' and 'constraint' of his middle years. Now the tapestry woven by these themes, or, to use Gide's beloved metaphor from Henry James, the figure in the carpet, is complete, and its name is 'Serenity'.

Gide's *Journal* was closed for ever. 'The above insignificant lines,' he wrote after a long pause on 25 January 1950, 'date from the 12th June 1949. Everything invites me to believe that they will be the last of this *Journal*.' But in the final autumn and winter of his life he felt the need to weave one more web of shot-silk tapestry from the threads of eighty years, and wrote *So Be It, or The Die is Cast*. His present condition is described, he says, by 'a very beautiful word, *anorexia,* meaning lack of appetite'. In fact not the least of the beauties of this ravishing book is the inter-mittent sense of extreme fatigue, the same as in the exultant white nights of Gide's youth, when he pressed his aching forehead on the window-pane and saw the Normandy dawn – except that now it is not sleep he resists, but death. Death, so be it, will come in a few months; meanwhile curiosity incessantly revives, anorexia is only a word, and the old man spreads out his mind like an espalier peach-tree against a sunny wall.

He has decided to write whatever comes into his head, without cheating, and while the topic changes on every page this master of construction makes the links seem both logical and undetectable. He examines his failing powers with unfailing power. He will recant nothing – 'as for the game I was playing, I have won it' – on the contrary, if he had his life over again he would have learned Greek, gone round the world four times, have yielded to even more temptations. He tells a series of absurdly funny stories, for this last portrait would be incomplete without his relish for the *saugrenu.* Then the revolving searchlight of his mind reaches further and further into his enormous past. On his return to Paris after the Liberation he found a complete outfit for forging identity papers hidden behind his dictionaries, no doubt by some Lafcadio of the Resistance; he remembers 'a dazzling red isolated flower' seen in the Caucasus on his visit to Soviet Russia, a moment of unhallowed bliss in his trip to the Congo, scenes from the Italian honeymoon of his never-consummated marriage, and deepest of all, across a gulf of seventy years, the secret games of his girl cousins at Rouen, when the inventive Valentine or bold Jeanne seemed more interesting than the timid Madeleine whom he married. In dreams, this author of *Oedipus* reveals, his dead wife's and dead mother's faces often change places, always 'with an inhibitory role'.

The hidden theme of this last testament is the quest for a final aphorism – 'believe those who seek the truth, doubt those who find it', he writes, but that is not it. 'Man's relations with God' ('this God', he remarks elsewhere, 'who awaits me, or so you say, and in whom I refuse to believe') 'have always seemed to me much more important and interesting than the relations of human beings with one another.' His last attempt, six days before death, the last words he wrote, is a formula of acceptance, the famous 'My own position in the sky, in relation to the sun, must not make me consider the dawn any less beautiful.'

He had planned to spend the coming spring in Marrakesh, as he had spent the last summer in Italy and Sicily. The success in December of his stage version of *The Vatican Swindle* at the Comédie Française, with two actors of genius, Jean Meyer and the ill-fated Roland Alexandre, as Protos and Lafcadio, had delighted and exhausted him. 'I had made no plans for being so old,' he wrote in *So Be It*. In February a lung infection brought an intolerable burden to his tired heart. Finding difficulty in expressing himself he said, with exquisite expression, 'I'm afraid my phrases may become grammatically inexact'; and a little later, when Cheyne-Stokes breathing had already set in: 'As always, it's the struggle between what is reasonable and what is not.' On 19 February 1951, late in the evening, came the last gratuitous act of death.

Most of Gide's critics bore the loss with fortitude, while his admirers mourned, in what seemed a darker, emptier world, an irreplaceable master and friend. Like his greater predecessors, Dante, Shakespeare, and Goethe, and his equals in his own century,

Proust and Joyce, he has constructed for his readers, in a life-work that is both universal and the consummation of his own epoch, a possible paradise that is unassailable by time and contingency. But Gide's paradise, and in this he is alone with Goethe, is earthly, on the hither side of sleep, time lost, and death. It is neither forfeited by tasting, nor gained by loss.

Gide did not believe in immortality; but in his works he has become, in a very real sense, immortal. His personality and his doctrine are preserved for ever; he will never cease to be what he was, to teach what he taught. He will continue to aid his fellow-creatures, the young and those who wish to remain young, the happy and those who wish to be happy, to live in courage and hope, and to achieve liberation and virtue. And if ever that dying quality, genius, returns to the world, Gide, as much as the greatest among his kin, will have helped it to free itself in youth and to remain productive and undespairing in old age.

SELECTIVE BIBLIOGRAPHY

A. WORKS BY ANDRÉ GIDE

I. COLLECTIONS

Œuvres complètes, 15 vols., Gallimard, Paris, 1932–9.
(This edition comprises Gide's published works up to 1929, and is also important as including many items – letters, articles, verses, prefaces, unfinished or minor works, etc. – uncollected or unpublished elsewhere. Its continuation is sometimes rumoured, and is much to be desired.)

Journal, 1889–1939, Bibliothèque de la Pléiade, Gallimard, Paris, 1939, 1941, 1949; includes also *La Marche Turque* and *Numquid et tu . . .?*
(*The Journals of André Gide*, trans. Justin O'Brien, 4 vols., Secker & Warburg, London, 1947–51; Knopf, New York, 1947–51. Vol. 4 comprises *Journal, 1939–1949.*)

Journal, 1939–49, Souvenirs, Bibliothèque de la Pléiade, Gallimard, Paris, 1954; includes also *Si le grain ne meurt . . ., Souvenirs de la cour d'assises, Voyage au Congo, Le Retour du Tchad, Carnets d'Égypte*, autobiographical essays from *Feuillets d'automne, Et Nunc Manet in Te, Ainsi soit-il*.

Romans, récits et soties, œuvres lyriques, Bibliothèque de la Pléiade, Gallimard, Paris, 1958; comprises *Le Traité du Narcisse, Le Voyage d'Urien, La Tentative amoureuse, Paludes, Les Nourritures terrestres, Les Nouvelles Nourritures, Le Prométhée mal enchaîné, El Hadj, L'Immoraliste, Le Retour de l'Enfant prodigue, La Porte étroite, Isabelle, Les Caves du Vatican, La Symphonie pastorale, Les Faux-Monnayeurs, L'École des femmes, Robert, Geneviève, Thésée.*

Théâtre: Saül, Le Roi Candaule, Œdipe, Perséphone, Le Treizième arbre, Gallimard, Paris, 1947.

II. SINGLE WORKS

1891 *Les Cahiers d'André Walter*, Librairie de l'Art Indépendant, Paris. (The Notebooks of André Walter.)

1892 *Le Traité du Narcisse*, Librairie de l'Art Indépendant, Paris. (*The Treatise of the Narcissus*, trans. Dorothy Bussy, as *Narcissus*, in *The Return of the Prodigal*, Secker & Warburg, London, 1953.)

Les Poésies d'André Walter, Librairie de l'Art Indépendant, Paris. (The Poems of André Walter.)

1893 *La Tentative amoureuse*, Librairie de l'Art Indépendant, Paris. (*The Attempt at Love*, trans. Dorothy Bussy, as *The Lovers' Attempt*, in *The Return of the Prodigal*, Secker & Warburg, London, 1953.)

Le Voyage d'Urien, Librairie de l'Art Indépendant, Paris. (*The Voyage of Urien*, trans. Wade Baskin, as *Urien's Voyage*, Peter Owen, London, 1964; Philosophical Library, New York, 1964.)

1895 *Paludes*, Librairie de l'Art Indépendant, Paris. (*Marshlands*, trans. George D. Painter, with *Prometheus Misbound*, Secker & Warburg, London, 1953; New Directions, New York, 1953.)

1897 *Les Nourritures terrestres*, Mercure de France, Paris. (*Fruits of the Earth*, trans. Dorothy Bussy, with *Later Fruits of the Earth*, Secker & Warburg, London, 1949; Knopf, New York, 1949.)

1899 *Philoctète*, Mercure de France, Paris. (*Philoctetes*, trans. Dorothy Bussy, in *The Return of the Prodigal*, Secker & Warburg, London, 1953; also trans. Jackson Mathews, in *My Theatre*, Knopf, New York, 1951.)

El Hadj, Mercure de France, Paris. (*El Hadj*, trans. Dorothy Bussy, in *The Return of the Prodigal*, Secker & Warburg, London, 1953.)

Le Prométhée mal enchaîné, Mercure de France, Paris. (*Prometheus Misbound*, trans. George D. Painter, in *Marshlands and Prometheus Misbound*, Secker & Warburg,

London, 1953; New Directions, New York, 1953; also
trans. Lady Lilian Rothermere, as *Prometheus Illbound*,
Chatto & Windus, London, 1919.)

1901 *Le Roi Candaule*, Revue Blanche, Paris.
(*King Candaules*, trans. Jackson Mathews, in *My Theater*,
Knopf, New York, 1951.)

1902 *L'Immoraliste*, Mercure de France, Paris.
(*The Immoralist,* trans. Dorothy Bussy, Cassell, London,
1930; Knopf, New York, 1930.)

1903 *Prétextes*, Mercure de France, Paris.
(*Pretexts*; selections from *Prétextes, Nouveaux Prétextes*
and *Incidences*, trans. Justin O'Brien, in *Pretexts*, Secker
& Warburg, London, 1959; Meridian, New York,
1959.)
Saül, Mercure de France, Paris.
(*Saul*, trans. Dorothy Bussy, in *The Return of the Prodigal*,
Secker & Warburg, London, 1953; also trans. Jackson
Mathews, in *My Theater*, Knopf, New York, 1951.)

1906 *Amyntas*, Mercure de France, Paris.
(*Amyntas*, trans. Villiers David, Bodley Head, London,
1958; Dufour, Chester Springs, Pa, 1961.)

1907 *Le Retour de l'Enfant prodigue*, Vers et Prose, Paris.
(*The Return of the Prodigal*, trans. Dorothy Bussy, with *Narcissus, The Lovers' Attempt, El Hadj, Philoctetes, Bathsheba,
Saul*, Secker & Warburg, London, 1953.)

1909 *La Porte étroite*, Mercure de France, Paris.
(*Strait is the Gate*, trans. Dorothy Bussy, Knopf, New York,
1924; Secker & Warburg, London, 1948.)

1910 *Oscar Wilde*, Mercure de France, Paris.
(*Oscar Wilde*, trans. Bernard Frechtman, Philosophical
Library, New York, 1949; Kimber, London, 1951.)

1911 *Isabelle*, N R F, Paris.
(*Isabelle*, trans. Dorothy Bussy, with *Pastoral Symphony*, in
Two Symphonies, Cassell, London, 1931, 1949; Knopf,
New York, 1931.)
Nouveaux Prétextes, Mercure de France, Paris.
(*New Pretexts*; selections, trans. Justin O'Brien, in *Pretexts*,

Secker & Warburg, London, 1959; Meridian, New York, 1959.)

1913   *Souvenirs de la cour d'assises*, NRF, Paris.
       (*Recollections of the Assize Court*, trans. Philip A. Wilkins, Hutchinson, 1941.)

1914   *Les Caves du Vatican*, NRF, Paris.
       (*The Vatican Swindle*, trans. Dorothy Bussy, Knopf, New York, 1925; also as *Lafcadio's Adventures*, Knopf, New York, 1927; as *The Vatican Cellars*, Cassell, London, 1952.)

1919   *La Symphonie pastorale*, NRF, Paris.
       (*Pastoral Symphony*, trans. Dorothy Bussy, in *Two Symphonies*, Cassell, 1931, 1949; Knopf, New York, 1931.)

1923   *Dostoïevsky*, Plon, Paris.
       (*Dostoevsky*, trans. anon, Dent, London, 1925, Knopf, New York, 1926; Secker & Warburg, London, 1949; New Directions, New York, 1949.)

1924   *Incidences*, Gallimard, Paris.
       (*Angles of Incidence*; selections, trans. Justin O'Brien, in *Pretexts*, Secker & Warburg, London, 1959; Meridian, New York, 1959.)
       Corydon, Gallimard, Paris.
       (*Corydon*, trans. P.B., Secker & Warburg, London, 1952; trans. Hugh Gibb, Farrer Strauss, New York, 1950.)

1926   *Les Faux-Monnayeurs*, Gallimard, Paris.
       (*The Coiners*, trans. Dorothy Bussy, as *The Counterfeiters*, Knopf, New York, 1927; as *The Coiners*, Cassell, London, 1950.)
       Le Journal des Faux-Monnayeurs, Gallimard, Paris.
       (*The Journal of 'The Coiners'*, trans. Justin O'Brien, as *The Logbook of The Coiners*, Cassell, London, 1952.
       Numquid et tu . . .?, Éditions de la Pléiade, Paris; also included in *Journal, 1889–1939*.
       (*Numquid et tu . . .?*, trans. Justin O'Brien, in *The Journals of André Gide*, vol. 2, Secker & Warburg, London, 1948; Knopf, New York, 1948.)
       Si le grain ne meurt . . ., Gallimard, Paris.

(*If It Die* . . ., trans. Dorothy Bussy, Random House, New
York, 1935; Secker & Warburg, London, 1951.)

1927   *Voyage au Congo*, Gallimard, Paris.
(*Travels in the Congo*, trans. Dorothy Bussy, with *Return
from Lake Chad*, Knopf, New York, 1929; Secker &
Warburg, London, 1930.)

1928   *Le Retour du Tchad*, Gallimard, Paris.
(*Return from Lake Chad*, trans. Dorothy Bussy, in *Travels in
the Congo*, Knopf, New York, 1929; Secker & Warburg,
London, 1930.)

1929   *L'École des femmes*, Gallimard, Paris; also, with *Robert* and
Geneviève, Gallimard, Paris, 1947.
(*The School for Wives*, trans. Dorothy Bussy, with *Robert*
and *Geneviève*, Cassell, London, 1950; Knopf, New
York, 1950.)
Robert, Gallimard, Paris.
(*Robert*, trans. Dorothy Bussy, in *The School for Wives*,
Cassell, London, 1950; Knopf, New York, 1950.)

1930   *L'Affaire Redureau*, Gallimard, Paris.
(The Redureau Case.)
La Séquestrée de Poitiers, Gallimard, Paris.
(The Prisoner of Poitiers.)

1931   *Œdipe*, Gallimard, Paris.
(*Oedipus*, trans. John Russell, in *Two Legends, Theseus and
Oedipus*, Secker & Warburg, London, 1950; Knopf,
New York, 1950.)

1934   *Perséphone*, Gallimard, Paris,
(*Persephone*, trans. Jackson Mathews, in *My Theater*,
Knopf, New York, 1951.)

1935   *Les Nouvelles Nourritures*, Gallimard, Paris.
(*Later Fruits of the Earth*, trans. Dorothy Bussy, in *Fruits of the
Earth*, Secker & Warburg, London, 1949; Knopf, New
York, 1949.)

1936   *Geneviève*, Gallimard, Paris.
(*Geneviève*, trans. Dorothy Bussy, in *The School for Wives*,
Cassell, London, 1950; Knopf, New York, 1950.)
Retour de l' U R S S, Gallimard, Paris.

(*Back from the U S S R*, trans. Dorothy Bussy, Secker & Warburg, London, 1937; Knopf, New York, 1937.)

1937   *Retouches à mon Retour de l 'U R S S*, Gallimard, Paris.
(*Afterthoughts on the U S S R*, trans. Dorothy Bussy, Secker & Warburg, London, 1937; Dial Press, New York, 1937.)

1946   *Thésée*, Gallimard, Paris.
(*Theseus*, trans. John Russell, in *Two Legends, Theseus and Oedipus*, Secker & Warburg, London, 1950; Knopf, New York, 1950.)
Hamlet (trans. of Shakespeare's *Hamlet*), Gallimard, Paris.
Le Retour, Ides et Calendes, Neuchâtel.
(The Return.)

1947   *Le Procès*, (a stage version of Kafka's *Der Prozess*, in collaboration with Jean-Louis Barrault), Gallimard, Paris.
(*The Trial*, trans. Jacqueline and Frank Sundstrom, Secker & Warburg, London, 1950; trans. Leon Katz, Schocken, New York, 1936.)

1948   *Notes sur Chopin*, L'Arche, Paris.
(*Notes on Chopin*, trans. Bernard Frechtman, Philosophical Library, New York, 1949.)
Francis Jammes et André Gide, Correspondance, 1893–1938, Gallimard, Paris.
(Correspondence with Francis Jammes.)

1949   *Feuillets d'automne*, Mercure de France, Paris.
(*Autumn Leaves*, trans. Elsie Pell, Philosophical Library, New York, 1950.)
Anthologie de la poésie française, Bibliothèque de la Pléiade, Gallimard, Paris.
(Anthology of French Poetry.)
Interviews imaginaires, Gallimard, Paris.
(*Imaginary Interviews*, trans. Malcolm Cowley, Knopf, New York, 1944.)
Paul Claudel et André Gide. Correspondance, 1899–1926, Gallimard, Paris.
(*The Correspondence between Paul Claudel and André Gide*,

trans. John Russell, Secker & Warburg, London, 1952;
Pantheon Books, New York, 1952.)

1950 *Littérature engagée*, Gallimard, Paris.
(Literature Takes Sides.)
Les Caves du Vatican, Farce en trois actes, Gallimard, Paris.
(The Vatican Cellars. A farce in three acts.)

1951 *Et Nunc Manet in Te*, Ides et Calendes, Neuchâtel.
(*Et Nunc Manet in Te*, trans. Justin O'Brien, Secker &
Warburg, London, 1953; as *Madeleine*, Knopf, New York,
1952.)

1952 *Ainsi soit-il, ou les Jeux sont faits*, Gallimard, Paris.
(*So Be It, or the Chips are Down*, trans. Justin O'Brien,
Knopf, New York, 1959; Chatto & Windus, London,
1960.)

1955 *André Gide – Paul Valéry, Correspondance, 1890–1942*,
Gallimard, Paris.
(Trans. and abridged by June Guicharnaud, as *Self-Portraits, the Gide–Valéry Letters*, University of Chicago
Press, Chicago, London, 1966.)

B. WORKS ON GIDE

ADAM, Antoine. 'Quelques années dans la vie d'André Gide', in
Revue des Sciences humaines, 1952, pp. 247–72.

ARCHAMBAULT, Paul. *Humanité d'André Gide*, Bloud and Gay,
Paris, 1946.

BRACHFELD, Georges I. *André Gide and the Communist Temptation*,
Librairie E. Droz, Geneva; Librairie Minard, Paris, 1959.

BRÉE, Germaine. *Gide*, Rutgers University Press, New Brunswick,
N.J., 1963.

COCTEAU, Jean. *Gide vivant*, Amiot Dumont, Paris, 1952.

DAVET, Yvonne. *Autour des Nourritures terrestres*, Gallimard, Paris,
1948.

DELAY, Jean. *La Jeunesse d'André Gide*, 2 vols., Gallimard, Paris,
1956, 57.
(*The Youth of André Gide*, trans. and abridged by June Guicharnaud, University of Chicago Press, Chicago, London, 1963.)

GUÉRARD, Albert J. *André Gide*, Harvard University Press, Cambridge, Mass; Oxford University Press, London, 1951.

IRELAND, G.W. *Gide*, Oliver & Boyd, Edinburgh and London; Grove Press, New York, 1963.

ISELER, Paul. *Les Débuts d'André Gide vus par Pierre Louÿs*, Éditions du Sagittaire, Paris, 1937.

LAFILLE, Pierre. *André Gide, romancier,* Hachette, Paris, 1954.

LAMBERT, Jean, *Gide familier,* Julliard, Paris, 1958.

MCLAREN, James C. *The Theater of André Gide*, Johns Hopkins Press, Baltimore; Oxford University Press, London, 1953.

MACHIAS, Claude, and HERBART, Pierre. *La Vie d'André Gide, album photographique*, Gallimard, Paris, 1955.

MARCH, Harold. *André Gide and the Hound of Heaven*, Pennsylvania University Press, Philadelphia; Oxford University Press, London, 1952.

MARTIN, Claude. *André Gide par lui-même*, Éditions du Seuil, Paris, 1963.

MARTIN DU GARD, Roger. *Notes sur André Gide*, Gallimard, Paris, 1951.
(*Notes on André Gide*, trans. John Russell, André Deutsch, London, 1953; as *Recollections of André Gide*, Viking Press, New York, 1953.)

NOUVELLE REVUE FRANÇAISE, special number. *Hommage à André Gide*, Gallimard, Paris, 1951.

O'BRIEN, Justin. *Portrait of André Gide*, Knopf, New York; Secker & Warburg, London, 1953.

PIERRE-QUINT, Léon. *André Gide*, Stock, Paris, 1932, 1952.

SCHLUMBERGER, Jean. *Madeleine et André Gide, leur vrai visage*, Gallimard, Paris, 1956.

STARKIE, Enid. *André Gide*, Bowes & Bowes, London; Yale University Press, New Haven, Conn., 1954.

GENERAL INDEX

INDEX OF WORKS

The page-numbers of the chief discussions of each work are given in heavy type

George D. Painter

George D. Painter's previous books include a monumental two-volume critical biography, *Proust: The Early Years* and *Proust: The Later Years*; a translation of Proust's *Letters to His Mother*; translations of André Gide's *Marshlands* and *Prometheus Misbound*; and a volume of poetry, *The Road to Sinodun*. His articles have appeared in *The Listener* and *The New Statesman*.